More Advance Praise for *On the Run*

"Every explosion has its ignition point, and the running explosion of the early seventies was no exception. Some will say it was Frank Shorter winning the Olympic Marathon, or Billy Rodgers winning Boston. But from where I stood, watching it all happen, it was a small-town high school kid named Joe Martino as much as anyone who ignited the art of running for the sheer exuberance of it. Savor Joe's story—you are in for a wild ride!"

— **Connie Putnam,**
head men's track and field/cross-country
coach (ret.), Tufts University

"Joe Martino is the true silent guardian of our sport. Having come through the 1960s-era of running, then competing in the first NYC Marathon (in 1970!) and bonding with legends and marathon champions Tom Fleming and Bill Rodgers, Joe's observations will be a welcome addition to the history of the sport we all love!"

— **Jeff Benjamin,**
senior writer, *The Running Network*

"Joe Martino is an exceptionally gifted individual in a variety of areas, with running and racing at the top of the list. Add to that Joe's remarkable communications ability, which makes every page of *On the Run* compelling reading—especially for anyone who has ever participated in track, cross-country, road races, or fun runs at any level."

— **Wayne Westcott,**
professor/director of exercise science, Quincy College

"Joe is a wonderful story-teller who makes you feel like you are part of the story. Great memories from the glory days of running."

— **Mickey Campaniello,**
Iron Man triathlete and Boston Marathon veteran

"Joe's memory and ability to tell stories is outstanding. Growing up in Greenfield, I watched and read about quite a few of his glorious moments. *On the Run* is such a fun read, and it takes me back to the days when Joe was my inspiration to start running."

— **Jeff Knapp,**
former model with the Click Agency, New York City

On the Run

Friendships & Finish Lines

Joe Martino

Copyright © 2020 by Joe Martino

All rights reserved. No part of this publication may be reproduced, distributed, or transmitted in any form or by any means, including recording, photocopying, or other digital, electronic or mechanical methods, without the prior written permission of the author.

Print ISBN: 978-1-7357994-0-7
Ebook ISBN: 978-1-7357994-1-4

Interior Layout by Amit Dey

Publisher's Cataloging-In-Publication Data
(Prepared by The Donohue Group, Inc.)
Names: Martino, Joe, 1952- author. | Rodgers, Bill, 1947- writer of supplementary textual content.
Title: On the run : friendships & finish lines / Joe Martino ; foreword by Bill Rodgers.
Description: [Medway, Massachusetts] : [Joe Martino], [2020] | Includes bibliographical references.
Identifiers: ISBN 9781735799407 (print) | ISBN 9781735799414 (ebook)
Subjects: LCSH: Martino, Joe, 1952—Career in marathon running. | Martino, Joe, 1952—Friends and associates. | Long-distance runners—United States—Biography. | Marathon running—United States—History—20th century. | New England—Social life and customs—20th century. | LCGFT: Autobiographies.
Classification: LCC GV1061.15.M357 A3 2020 (print) | LCC GV1061.15. M357 (ebook) | DDC 796.42092—dc23

Cover photo taken during the Johnny Kelly Half-Marathon, in Hyannis Massachusetts, May 31, 1982.

To my wife, Ginger, for her love,
support, and encouragement:
thank you for being on this adventure with me.

To my dad, Joe, for being a great role model
and always being there.

> For though my life's been good to me,
> there's still so much to do,
> so many things my mind has never known.
>
> **—John Denver,**
> *Poems, Prayers and Promises*

Contents

Foreword by Bill Rodgers. ix
Introduction xiii
1. Greenfield 1
2. Cross-Country 11
3. Senior Year 17
4. Holyoke Massacre 29
5. Twenty-Four-Hour Relay 35
6. New York City Marathon 39
7. They Called Me Coach 43
8. Hollywood 49
9. São Paulo Dream 55
    Photos 61
10. Cemetery 85
11. Polish Picnic 89
12. The Rookie 93
13. The Marathon 99

14. Oasis in the Winter	109
15. To Finish Is to Win	115
16. Camping	121
17. Millrose Games	127
18. Tom Fleming	133
19. Toast to the Ones We Lost	139
20. Laughing All the Way	149
21. The Finish Line	153
Running Résumé	159
Acknowledgments	161
About the Author	165

Foreword

One Sunday in the summer of 1985 I was meeting my friend Tom Fleming to go on a twenty-mile run to Boston College at the top of Heartbreak Hill, the famous Boston Marathon landmark. When Tom walked up my driveway, I saw he'd brought a friend with him. Little did I know that the three of us—Tom, Joe, and myself—would soon be calling ourselves "The Three Amigos" and form a tight-knit friendship that would last a lifetime.

At the time Joe was already an accomplished runner. A fierce competitor, he'd run undefeated in dual meets in both track and cross-country in his senior year of high school. That was 1969. The following year, he ran the Holyoke Marathon—the "Holyoke Massacre," as they used to call it—and a few months after that ran the very first New York City Marathon and took thirteenth place.

Back then exercise science and sports nutrition were still in their infancy, and the sport of road running was not much different from what it was in 1896, when the first modern Olympics were held in Athens, Greece. There were no cash prizes, no big press, no fame, no national accolades; most runners' central goal came down to seeing if they could beat their own record and become just *that* much better.

A hundred twenty-six participants went to the starting line that hot and humid September day. This year, more than *fifty thousand* runners would have come to participate in the race's fiftieth anniversary, had it not been canceled for the first time in its history, due to the COVID-19 outbreak.

Over the years following that summer Sunday in 1985 I traveled to Joe's hometown of Greenfield, Mass, a number of times, and couldn't help noticing how obvious it was that Joe was such a well-known fixture in the community. It seemed like everywhere we went, people knew him. Even today, all these years later, when I travel to races around the country people tell me they were a friend of Joe Martino's and to please say hello.

Ample testimony to the fact that Joe is not only a great athlete, but a great human being, too.

A few years after we met, Joe moved into my carriage house in Dover, Mass. Every morning I'd go knock on his door and we'd go put on the miles together.

One spring morning I was scheduled to run a half-marathon in Danbury, Connecticut, a good three-hour drive from my place. As Joe puts it, I have "a reputation for cutting it close, time-wise." About three hours before the race was to start, I climbed into the car with my wife and daughter and we headed off toward the Mass Pike.

About ten minutes later, Joe heard a loud pounding on his door. "Joe! Joe!" At the time my wife's Aunt Helen was staying with us, and Joe opened the door to find Aunt Helen standing there, staring at him. She was frantic.

"Joe, this is terrible! Bill left for the race—and he took *my* bag by mistake!"

My running bag contained my running clothes and shoes. Aunt Helen's, of course, contained *hers*. Which meant the Danbury

Half-Marathon's special out-of-town guest would be soon arriving…without any shoes or clothes.

Joe's mind raced. He knew there was no hope of catching up to us on the road to the Pike, with our ten-minute head start. This was years before anyone owned cell phones. There was no way to reach me.

He grabbed the house phone and dialed the Massachusetts Turnpike Authority. "My name's Joe Martino—hey, do you know who Bill Rodgers is?"

"You mean the runner?" said the guy.

Yes, Joe meant *that* Bill Rodgers.

Joe explained what had happened, described my car, and said I would be passing through the Natick toll booth, heading west to Connecticut, in the next few minutes.

The guy jumped into action. He contacted every toll-taker in every booth at the Natick station, told them I was coming, and that whoever saw me first needed to stop the car and explain the situation.

Joe and Aunt Helen sat outside my house, as nervous as any expectant father pacing the waiting room.

When I pulled up twenty minutes later, his face broke into a look of relief I'll never forget. Without a word I jumped out, grabbed the right bag, and we were off.

Joe has always run a heck of a strong race—but that day it was his fast thinking that saved my hide!

For nearly a quarter-century the Three Amigos ran together, celebrated together, and had all kinds of memorable experiences together. Then, on April 19, 2017, we got the devastating news that Tom Fleming had passed away.

We were all in a state of shock. Tom had such a great heart, and his passing left us broken and speechless. The memorial service was held at Montclair Kimberly Academy, in New Jersey, where Tom was a teacher and coach. The auditorium was standing room only, jam packed with Tom's family and friends, students and fellow teachers. The overflow watched a live-stream of the service from the school's cafeteria. The world running community was well represented, too, with people like George Hirsch, Jeff Benjamin, Bobby Hodge, Dan and Patti Dillon, Mike Roche and John McGrath among those who came to honor one of America's greatest marathon runners, and one of our greatest friends.

Everyone there was in a state of grief and disbelief. Tom was bigger than life; it didn't seem possible that he could be gone.

My New Year always kicks off with Joe and his wife Ginger's legendary New Year's Day open house. It's a wonderful event, being there to enjoy Ginger's famous homemade chili and the company of great friends. Tom would always be there, lighting up the room. I knew it would never be quite the same again.

Joe and I were asked to speak at the service. I was so shattered I could hardly find the words—but Joe got up and spoke, telling stories that beautifully and vividly evoked Tom the way he was, so full of life and energy. He brought Tom to life and made us all laugh out loud. It was the perfect testament to a great friend— *from* a great friend.

As he did that day at Tom's memorial, Joe captures so many of these stories so well in the pages of *On the Run*. His memory for details is uncanny, and his stories capture so much about the history of running and racing in the sixties and right up through the nineties. During all our adventures together, Joe has always been the glue, bringing us all together and looking for that next great story.

I hope you enjoy reading *On the Run* as much as I did.

See you on the roads,
Bill Rodgers

Introduction

"Oh, the places you'll go!"

—Dr. Seuss

I grew up in Greenfield, Massachusetts, a small town in the western part of the state, just a few miles south of the Vermont border. As a child, sports and physical activity played big roles in my life. If I wasn't at the Beacon Field tennis courts, you could find me at the local Y.

My father first took my younger brother Greg and me to the YMCA in 1961 when we were six and eight years old. He enrolled all three of us in Jim Allen's judo program. Over the next few years, my father would compete in judo matches all over New England, winning the New England Judo Championship in 1965. Along with judo, Greg and I attended swimming lessons and a Saturday program at the Y, which involved swimming, gym activities, and a movie, while eating our bagged lunches in the youth building.

Over those four years the Y became an everyday after-school activity. I would walk to the Y after school dismissal with my two buddies, Dave Siano and Gary Burniski. At school, we had to talk in code, trying to keep our destination secret from the nuns who were our teachers at Holy Trinity. The nuns didn't understand what the Y was and they were suspicious of its Protestant connotations.

When I was twelve my mother passed away, and the Y became my second home. Losing my mom at a young age was devastating. My Aunt Ann chipped in as often as she could but my father needed a refuge as he raised two young boys by himself. So the Y became our extended family, with Jim Allen, the physical director at the Y, as a second father. Jim would remain a close friend until his death in 2000.

As a young teen I joined the YMCA Leaders Club, eventually becoming its president. Leaders Club taught skills that prepared us to assist teaching classes with younger children. Through the club, I met Frank McDonald, Michele Couture, and Ruth Ann Burt. Today, fifty-four years later, Frank remains a close friend. Michele and I always joked about being brother and sister; we remain dear friends to this day. And Ruth Ann, now Ana Gabriel Mann, has helped me with this book.

After spending most of my young life at the Y, I worked on the staff at the Y camp and became a Y fitness volunteer. The place grew from a second home to a source of passion and dedication. So it seemed logical to make working for the Y my long-term career choice. In 2016 I retired after thirty-four years as a Y professional.

In addition to spending much of my childhood at the Y, I also took summer tennis lessons with Rich Kells, the local tennis guru and president of the Greenfield tennis club. Mark Fotopulos and I met at tennis lessons and were soon on the courts together for hours daily, sometimes twice a day. We would often practice all morning, ride our bikes home for lunch, and then head back to the courts in the afternoon.

We began competing in tennis tournaments locally and around the state. Mark became a ranked player in the twelve-and-under division and I did the same in the fourteen-and-under. In our early teens, Mark and I started beating the players on the high school team. It was funny seeing how frustrated it made some of the older players to be beaten by a couple of cocky young kids.

All that to say: running was not my first athletic love—but it became my deepest.

I got hooked on running in 1966, during my first run in Highland Park. My Leaders Club buddy Frank McDonald was on the high school cross-country team and encouraged me to join. I ran my first road race at fourteen, two four-mile loops in Granby that almost killed me. I finished in thirty-second place, but the challenge gave me a big sense of accomplishment.

I craved more.

My high school running career began in the fall of 1967, running cross-country as a sophomore. During 1967 and 1968, Frank and I ran together almost every day, sometimes twice a day. On occasion, I would even sneak in a third run.

It's hard to express how much I loved being a runner. I had fun. I gained confidence. I felt good about myself. Running became a core part of my identity—and I worked harder at it than anybody I knew.

I'm proud of my high school running accomplishments. It was great winning Western Mass titles and finishing second in the state meet. Perhaps the most satisfying award I received in high school was being voted by my senior classmates as "Most Athletic." It really pissed off the football, baseball, and basketball players who traditionally won the title. Another win for running!

During the running boom of the late 1970s, I worked at Clark's Sport Shop in Greenfield. Clark's was a high-quality sporting goods store owned by Don Clark. Don was very supportive of the local running community, often sponsoring races and donating prizes to events. Don generously supported me as a runner with shoes and clothing. Clark's became a favorite drop-in spot for local runners looking for gear and running advice.

Running, tennis, and the Y were through roads that led me from being a heartbroken kid to being a competitive teenager and then a focused man. This book is a way to share my memories of how these activities shaped my life.

I've always enjoyed telling stories. Whether I'm sharing stories over a beer or over Facebook, my family and friends have often encouraged me to write them down and put them in a book. Doing so has been a great exercise for me, and has pushed me way beyond my comfort zone. While I enjoy telling stories, I'm admittedly not a writer. (My high school English teachers, Olive Corbiere, Marilyn Munn, and Dick Russo, would be quite surprised to see this book appear.)

I wrote this book for several reasons.

First, I wanted to leave a legacy for my children and grandchildren and other family members who were not around to witness this important part of my life.

I also wanted a forum to express my thanks to the many people who have played such a big part of this extraordinary life I have been blessed to live.

Finally, I wanted to tell stories of the way it was, and hopefully bring out a memory and a smile or two for those who read this account.

Material from this book comes exclusively from my memory, along with my collection of running log books, most of which I still have.

Having good stories is helped by having good friends. I am so fortunate to count Tom Fleming and Bill Rodgers as friends and brothers. We called ourselves "The Three Amigos" and ran, traveled, and played together every chance we got, and that has added up to countless adventures, laughs, and memories.

Life up to this point has been an amazing journey and I've met some of the best people I could ever imagine along the way.

—Joe Martino,
October 2020

1

Greenfield

I played a lot of golf three summers ago with my childhood friend, Jamie O'Neil. Jamie and I grew up together, beginning with our early days at Holy Trinity School. Jamie was a fantastic athlete who could do just about anything. He played high-quality tennis, was an excellent basketball player, and was a top-notch juggler and magician. In fact, Jamie and our mutual friend Mickey Campaniello teamed up and juggled professionally as "Pencil and Stencil the Clowns."

In the early seventies, Jamie and I lived together in an attic apartment with two other guys. The apartment had one bedroom, two cubby-hole storage spaces which we made into bedrooms, and a living room with a pullout couch. We were quite a collection of characters. Larss Ogren was one of the county's best all-around athletes. Mike "Kack" Kachelmeyer was a high school basketball star from Batavia, New York. Kack could do magical things with a basketball.

When Jamie joined the National Guard to avoid getting drafted, my high school friend and trackmate Rick Sherlund moved in. Rick was a postgrad student at Deerfield Academy and was supposed to be living with our high school track coach. Despite our bad influence, constant parties, and people regularly dropping by, Rick turned out amazingly successful. Rick would go on to earn an MBA at Cornell University and embark on a long career as a software analyst with Goldman Sachs.

Some of my fondest memories of Jamie revolved around music. He played great guitar and could sing. He was always introducing me to new music by emerging artists such as Eric Anderson, Thirty Days Out, Tom Rush, Steve Goodman, and Tom Waits.

Despite not having a college degree, Jamie was an incredible success story. After starting out as a supply clerk at the nuclear power plant in Vernon, Vermont, Jamie moved up the ladder and worked at several corporations before starting his own business, Impact Skillsets, Inc. Jamie's business provided management training for company employees throughout the country. His intelligence, interpersonal skills, and natural leadership abilities were the foundation of his success.

Jamie was a member of a country club in Kingston, Massachusetts. Indian Pond was a gorgeous golf course, always in immaculate condition. I felt so privileged to be playing at Jamie's club, which was way out of my economic bracket. Jamie was an excellent golfer, often shooting in the high seventies. (I was trying hard to break 100.) Jamie loved to teach and I learned something new at every outing. He was constantly reminding me to keep my head down and to finish my swing.

One beautiful September afternoon at Indian Pond stands out in memory. The course was in great shape and the greens were very fast. Jamie shot a seventy-seven and I shot my all-time best of ninety-four. Jamie's score really impressed me, given the circumstances. The previous summer, Jamie had been diagnosed with a stomach cancer. The treatments were physically taxing and left him feeling exhausted.

But he could still handle a golf club.

I'll always remember the twelfth tee, which was located on a hillside. The elevated tee box provided an amazing view of the golf course; it was simply breathtaking. The hole itself was intimidating, with a lake to the left of the green, bunkers around it, and trees on the right side. The course was backed up with people waiting to play, and that was slowing down play, so Jamie and I stood together quietly on the tee box, taking in the awesome beauty. All of a sudden Jamie turned to me, smiled, and said, "Not bad for a couple of guys from Greenfield."

Not bad, Jamie, not bad at all.

Greenfield was a wonderful place to grow up, especially if you were a runner. Several of my running routes were as nice as anyplace I've run in the country. The landscape was spectacular with countless running opportunities. Hills were abundant and there were also places to run on the flats.

My favorite place to run in the summer was along the Green River. I would park at the top of the pumping station road and head out onto the river road into Colrain. That road is hard-packed dirt. The first time Tom Fleming ran the river with me he asked, "What's this?" The Jersey boy wasn't sure what surface he was running on. I laughed as I told him, "Tom, it's dirt!"

My course was five miles out, with the turnaround at the Ten Mile Bridge and then five miles back. The road was shaded and it was much cooler running along the river than running in town on a hot summer day. There was a refreshing spring where cold water shot out from a pipe someone had pounded into a crevasse. I always stopped there for a drink on the way out and again on the return trip. Along the way, the views of the river were picturesque. I'd wheel-measured the course for accuracy and painted mile markers on trees and rocks.

You could modify the river road course depending on how far you wanted to run. It was five miles from my apartment in town to the start of the road, which made for a perfect twenty-mile out-and-back run. For a twelve-miler, I would start at my father's house, which was exactly one mile from the river. If I really wanted a tough run, I could make the course fifteen miles by starting at my father's house, crossing the Ten Mile Bridge, then taking a three-mile loop back to the bridge. The loop involved a one-and-a-half-mile climb towards the town of Leyden. The views were amazing; you could see all the way to the University of Massachusetts in Amherst and beyond.

It was on this fifteen-mile course that I once thought my cardiovascular system might explode.

I'd taken Bill Rodgers to my folks' home in Greenfield to show him where I grew up. I thought he might like to run the fifteen-miler. It was a hot day and we were running about six-minute miles. We began the hill climb at the six-mile mark, shortening our stride but still keeping a fast pace. Nearing the peak of the mountain, I felt as though my cardiovascular system had reached maximum. I could count my heart rate without even touching my body, just by feeling the strong beating in my chest. I talked Bill into slowing down so I could recover. It was one of the toughest fifteen-mile runs I've ever been on.

My favorite run in town was The Ridge, a wooded, pine-needle path that ran uphill for about a mile and a half and ended at Poet's Seat Tower. The view from the peak was panoramic. You could see the entire town of Greenfield and all the surrounding area. It was at that spot, after our high school graduation, that Pete Wayman, Rick Sherlund, and I decided to give the town a pre-Fourth-of-July fireworks exhibition. We lined about thirty rockets on the rock wall on the edge of the cliff and began lighting them off.

It was a great fireworks demonstration...until we saw the flashing lights of a police cruiser coming up the access road. Pete took off in his car and Rick and I jumped down into an area of thick brush, hiding behind two large rocks. We could hear the voices coming through the cruiser's radio as the bright beams from police flashlights lit up the area just behind us. After about ten minutes they gave up the search, and Rick and I made our way down the mountain to our car.

From The Ridge, you could connect to Highland Park, which was the home of our high school's cross-country course. Our course was the toughest one I ever ran on. It also pushed the less-than-three-mile rule for high school courses. I think it clocked in at 2.999 miles when measured in straight lines! In my three years at Highland Park, I never lost a single home meet.

It was a wonderful area to run, with endless possibilities—and was right in town.

Over the years, Frank McDonald and I competed in road races all over New England. Eventually we had a thought: "Why not have a road race right here in Greenfield?" We spoke to Walter and Dick Childs, who were officials for the local Western Massachusetts Amateur Athletic Union (AAU). The AAU controlled running and was the sanctioning body for all road races. Things moved faster than Frank and I expected. Before we had a chance to go over the details with Jim Allen (the physical director at the Y,) the Greenfield race was already on the schedule. A real stickler for organization, Jim was caught a little off guard. After assuring him that we could do this, the Y agreed to run the event and Jim became the race director. Clark's Sport Shop was the race sponsor.

On April 27, 1968, the first Greenfield race attracted forty-one entrants. George Conefrey (running for the Brockton Athletic Club) won. Fifteen-year-old me finished in ninth place, out-sprinting Dr. Charlie Robbins, who was a veteran runner of the New York Pioneer Club and was well-known for running barefoot.

That race also marked a return to yesteryear, as Greenfield had served as host to some major New England road races back in the early 1950s.

The Greenfield race was a big hit and became an annual event for more than twenty years. Hundreds of residents lined the six-mile course, supporting the runners and handing out water. It was Greenfield's version of the Boston Marathon. In fact, the date always conflicted with the Boston Marathon, and I always chose to run Greenfield. I trained and tried to win Greenfield more than any other race. But some stud runner would always show up—John Dimick, Ken Kaczenski, Tom Derderian, or Jack Mahurin, to name a few—and bump me from my goal. Over the years, I finished in the top ten a total of eleven times, including one second-place, four thirds, three fourths, and two fifths.

Poet Seat Ridge Runners was an offshoot of the Greenfield Y road race, founded by Ed and Paul Porter. The Amherst area had the Sugarloaf Mountain Athletic Club and Pittsfield organized the Berkshire Hill Runners. It was time for a Greenfield running group! The Ridge Runners were a great bunch of people who loved to run and really enjoyed the social aspect of the sport. (That's a respectable way to say there seemed to be a party attached to most Ridge Runner events!) Dedicated Ridge Runners included Bette Richard, Maureen Casey, Jack McKenzie, Carry Crossman, Anne and Scott Lyman, Ed and Corleen Porter, Paul and Liz Porter, Sherry

MacAdam, Roger Reid, Lou Socquet, Cheryl Carley, and Mickey Campaniello.

Plus me, of course. But after a while with the Ridge Runners, I longed for more competition, so I joined the Greater Boston Track Club and competed in several events for the GBTC over that year. Looking back, I should have stayed with the Ridge Runners. I lived two hours from Boston and never socially connected with many GBTC runners. I eventually ended up running with The Greater Springfield Harriers and had the opportunity to compete as a team member in several national championships.

Although I often trained alone, there was always someone who wanted to run together. Roger Reid was lean and fit and a naturally gifted runner. Roger, a lawyer, lives on a mountaintop in Ashfield, Massachusetts, in the middle of nowhere. Roger brought me to my first wine tasting in Northampton. My previous experience with wine was Boone's Farm Apple Blossom. At that Northampton wine tasting, I remember Roger telling me, "When they pour you a glass, don't swig it down." I always think of that night when I'm in France in some winemaker's cellar tasting something special.

One April night after a run, Roger and I went to the local discount store called Railroad Salvage, across the river in Turners Falls. A very thrifty guy, Roger liked to browse through what I would call junk. Leaving the store on the mild early spring evening, the Connecticut River was really high and roaring from the spring thaw.

As we stepped into the car, I thought I heard a voice coming from the distance. We got out and walked towards the raging river and listened again. We thought we heard a call for help but we couldn't figure out where it came from. We got into the car and drove to the other side of the river. There, we could clearly hear the cry for help. The fire department arrived and we all went down the soggy wooded embankment to the edge of a rocky cliff. With the flashlights from the firemen, we could see a guy clinging to the rocks in the water, shivering badly.

After assessing the situation, Roger, the lightest of the bunch, was chosen to be harnessed in and lowered down to put a rope around the guy. Roger was up for the challenge. Eventually, we pulled both Roger and the man up to safety. Apparently, the guy jumped into the water to commit suicide but changed his mind as he was floating down the ice-cold river.

After the rescue, we headed to my apartment to watch the Celtics playoff game. We weren't at my place more than five minutes when the phone rang; the local news media wanted a comment. The next day, Roger had his picture in the newspaper with an article describing his heroics…and I broke out in a wicked case of poison ivy. I like to think Roger and I both made heroic sacrifices for the good of our fellow man that April night.

In 1970, Frank McDonald tried to persuade the town of Greenfield to hold summer fun runs at Highland Park. The model was based on weekly cross-country races held in the summer at Forest Park in Springfield. Frank received approval and a small budget to cover the cost of ribbons for the winners. The Run for Fun finishers would receive numbered popsicle sticks to coordinate their finish place with their time. The first run, we had sixteen individuals, and each week it grew. During the first two years we saw about thirty to forty participants each week.

The third year, when Frank headed off to boot camp to become a Marine Corps officer, I took over Run for Fun. The event grew, and we started a kids' runs for all ages. Frank's cousin Paul McDonald ran with his family. Kathy McDonald competed in the eight-and-under category and Kelly McDonald ran in the five-and-under. Frank and Mary Fitz ran along with their daughter, Betsy. Monday night regulars included Bette Richard, Mike Lorden, Dick Townsley, and Larry Saczawa. Every week, Bill and Linda Batty attended with their three children: John in the five-and-under, Rocky in the six-and-under, and Mary in the eight-and-under. It seemed like half the town ran every Monday evening! Even Irving, the Ding Dong man, showed up. Each week, Irving would pull into the parking lot in his ice cream truck, close up the truck, and appear in his running clothes ready to race. It wasn't uncommon to have fifty people in that Monday night run.

In the mid-seventies, Run for Fun grew even bigger. Pete Duffy, the Y youth director, urged his Camp Apex staff to attend as a team-building exercise. Attendance grew to over a hundred each week. Pete ran along with most of his camp staff and his daughters named Colleen, Pam, and Amy. Paul Seamans became a regular, along with his daughter, Susan. Several members of the Knapp family ran, including Becca and Katie. Katie became a runner on my junior high school team and went on to run very well in high school. My dear friend Michele Couture ran along with her sister Karen, Becky Folta, and Susan Widdison. My sister Tammy Bemis ran each week along with Mary Ann Marsh. The Cahill sisters, Linda and Debbie, would be there, running for fun. Other regulars were Mike and Ellen Kelton, who came with their daughter Gretchen. The list of families enjoying a free, healthy event all summer long goes on and on.

Despite its name, Run for Fun was a very competitive event. I loved the fast 2.2-mile course and held the record for several years. Some top runners showed up, including Tom Derderian, Ed Sandifer, and Tony Wilcox. Amherst High School stars like Dan Newell jumped in from time to time. Dick Hoyt (of Rick and Dick Hoyt future fame) came and enjoyed the competition. My high school coach Pete Conway began his comeback at Run for Fun. Some of New England's finest women distance runners also competed. Charlotte Lettis and Merry Cushing ran a number of times. In the forty-and-over division, Ray Willis and Paul Seamans competed on a regular basis. One evening, Greenfield High School sprint/hurdle star Chris Ryan ran, testing himself on the longer distance. Afterward, Chris decided that he'd best stick to hurdles.

After the race finished, a group of us always went out for an easy four-to-six-mile run. The warm-down run was one of the best parts of the evening. A pack of ten or so of us running together, chatting about training, and just plain catching up.

Being from a small town meant that whenever you went for a run, you saw people you knew. During a typical in-town run, you'd have at least half a dozen cars tooting their horn to say "Hi." When my wife, Ginger, first visited Greenfield with me in the late eighties, she told me it reminded her of *Mr. Rogers' Neighborhood*. As we walked down Main Street, she was amazed at all the people I knew and stopped to chat with. This was eighteen years after high school!

My Greenfield training runs took me down East Cleveland Street, where Mr. Graves, the high school custodian, would greet me from his front yard. The same thing happened daily with Mr. Benjamin, my junior high gym teacher, who was always on his porch in the afternoon. Mr. Benjamin's house would usually require a quick stop and chat. He's the person who encouraged me to go out for cross-country in ninth grade. I remember seeing Mr. Dejoy on his daily walks and Mr. Ninos from the Pizza Patch waving to me from inside his store. If it was an early evening run, I could always count on seeing Dr. and Mrs. McDonald sitting out on the porch on the corner of Federal and Maple, listening to the Red Sox Game.

I feel so fortunate to have grown up in Greenfield. I had a close family, great friends, and a wonderful support system. I could not think of a better place to grow up as a runner.

2

Cross-Country

Fall means something different to everyone. For me, when the fall season comes, I think of cross-country.

It's something about the cool air and the warm sun. The fall foliage with its colorful leaves covering the running trail make the cross-country course feel magical. The terrain of forest, fields, trails, and hills all challenge you. It's so different from running on the roads or a track.

I remember the first time I heard about cross-country. I was twelve or thirteen years old and in my father's car, on River Road in Deerfield. My father slowed down as we passed a group of high school boys running. I asked my father what they were doing and he said they were cross-country runners and they ran long distances.

My second encounter was in 1964 on a late summer afternoon at the Beacon Field tennis courts. I was playing tennis with my friend Mark Fotopulos when a group of runners came across the field and stopped at the courts for a drink of water. I remember thinking how fit they looked and being amazed at the fact that they didn't even seem to be tired. After a brief water break, off they went, back towards the high school. I'd later learn that these runners were part of the 1964 Greenfield High School state championship cross-country team! I had no idea I was going to be a cross-country runner, but I think the seed was planted back then.

I began running after my freshman year football season in 1966. I realized there was no future for me in football, as sitting on the bench was no fun. I was a good athlete, active at the Y, and I just about lived on the tennis courts from an early age. My gym teacher, Stan Benjamin, noticed when we ran laps in gym class, I always finished ahead of my classmates. (Lots of kids went out really fast and then struggled to get to the finish.) He encouraged me to go out for cross-country. One of my classmates, Gary Underwood, took me for a run to Highland Park and introduced me to the cross-country course.

It was a sunny, cool day at the peak of foliage. The paths were covered in pine needles in some places, and in other spots, with colorful leaves. And the smell! The fresh air and feel of the warm sun on a cool fall day was intoxicating. The act of running up and down hills, the beautiful winding forest trails, and even the term "cross-country" had an instant appeal to me.

I was hooked. When football ended, I began running every day after school, preparing for the fall of my sophomore year: the beginning of high school cross-country.

Our first cross-country meet was on Friday, September 28, 1967. We ran a dual meet against Mohawk Regional. Despite having never run a cross-country race before, I felt confident from all the road races I'd run over the summer. I had trained in Highland Park almost daily. The course was soggy and muddy, due to several days of soaking rain. I won the race by forty-five seconds, beating Mohawk's top runner, Tom Benz. My teammate Don Bassett finished a close third to Tom, and the rest of our team—Tim Duprey, Larry Garland, Frank McDonald, and Peter Winn—all finished strong. We won the meet by three points in front of about ten spectators.

The next morning I got out of bed and went into the kitchen for breakfast. On the table was the morning newspaper, the *Greenfield Recorder*. Hoping to see if the race results from our first meet were included, I quickly turned to the sports page. I was totally stunned to see the caption, "Greenfield Tips Mohawk with Surprise Attack" along with *my picture*. My own performance hadn't surprised me that much, as I knew how hard I'd worked the previous eleven months. Seeing my picture in the paper, though, that had a profound effect on me.

I'd had my picture in the news several times before as a youngster playing in tennis tournaments, but this was the first recognition of my new passion, distance running. My friends and fellow students noticed, and cross-country began getting some attention. My confidence level grew stronger and it drove me to train harder.

Preparing for my first cross-country season, I often trained with my friend Frank McDonald. Frank was also interested in running road races and we would participate in them every chance we got. Frank would borrow his parents' car and off we'd go to run a race in some small town in Western Mass. One time, we were dropped off at a race near Worcester by Frank's sister and hitchhiked home.

Road racing gave me strength, experience, and confidence. I met many great runners who enjoyed sharing their training programs with me. Ed Walkwitz, John Jarek, Roland Cormier, and Tom Derderian were all road runners I learned from. I joined a running club, the Mountain Park Athletic Association, and competed in the off-season. I went on a few training runs with Dave Ciszewski, who it turned out was the leader of that championship running group I'd seen stopping for a water break at the tennis courts a few years before. Dave was one tough competitor and was years ahead of his time.

As a high school team, we tried to build excitement and generate interest in our sport. One strategy was to wear our running shoes to school on the days of our meets. There was a dress code that forbade wearing sneakers to school. But when we wound up in the principal's office to plead our case to Mr. Jones, we were ready. We'd brought a Ontisuka Tiger shoebox with us that said "running shoes" on the front. "See? We aren't wearing sneakers," we said. "We're wearing running shoes!" Mr. Jones made an exception…which we pushed to the limit. Not long after that, everyone began wearing sneakers and running shoes to school. We created a revolution!

Our cross-country course was the toughest one in Western Mass. Supposedly, it was measured at 2.99 miles and was the creation of Pete Conway, my future coach. You had to know how to run it strategically, which made it a definite home-course advantage for us.

Located two miles from the high school in Highland Park, the course ran mostly flat for three quarters of a mile on a dirt road, then slightly uphill to the mile mark, which was on a narrow winding trail with no room to pass. You next had a short but very demanding climb up a rocky path under the high tension wires. Then you went down the steepest drop-off I've ever run. The park road led to Mountain Road (appropriately named) before rolling down the other side of the mountain to the north entrance of the park. A long straightaway led to a sharp turn onto a trail over a wooden bridge and up a grassy hill, with a fast three hundred meters to the finish line.

The course record was held by Al Stevens, a Keene, New Hampshire, runner who ran 15:54 in 1965. I finally broke the record in 1969, running 15:47 on my very last try.

Over those three years at Highland Park, I was never beaten. The closest race I ever had was my senior year. Bobby Williams was an unbelievable talent for Pioneer Valley Regional High School. The year prior, Bob had beaten me for the Western Mass title. He was a freshman and had an amazing natural ability. We trained together for a bit in the summer and he knew the course well.

Both our teams, along with Bobby and me as individuals, were unbeaten. The *Greenfield Recorder* built up the race with two articles talking about the two undefeated runners and two undefeated schools. Spectators showed up. My teammate's girlfriend was a cheerleader, and I remember watching a school van pull up with the entire cheering squad. So much for the loneliness of the long-distance runner!

Pete Conway came up with a race strategy for me, though he wouldn't officially become my coach until the winter track season. Pete said to go out hard the first mile, recover, and then work Mountain Road really hard. "If Bobby's still with you when you roll down the other side," he said, "then we've got a problem." Pete told me to watch for him during the race. He'd be holding a white towel and when he dropped the towel, no matter how far from the finish or how badly I felt, I needed to, in Pete's words, "Go as hard as you can for as long as you can."

Sure enough, I couldn't shake Bobby during the race. I knew he had much better finishing speed than I did. I could feel him on my shoulder and hear his steps. I saw Pete about six hundred yards from the finish, holding the white towel. When I got close, he dropped the towel and off I went with everything I had. The move stunned Bobby and he didn't react at first. When he did, it was too late for him. I won by thirty-two seconds and our team remained undefeated.

Cross-country suited me well and I found success with it. I only lost once as a sophomore and once as a junior. I never lost a race on my home course. When I *did* lose, I trained harder. As a senior, I won the Western Mass All Division meet, after finishing second the year before.

Throughout my running career, I enjoyed running road races, marathons, indoor track, and outdoor track. I have great memories of all of them but cross-country remains special.

Even today, I always think of cross-country in the fall.

3

Senior Year

The spring of 1970 was an exciting time. It was my senior year of high school, post-graduation plans were being made, and our final track season was just getting underway. The Kinks were singing "Lola" on the radio, *Gunsmoke* was on TV, and *Love Story* was playing at the movie theater.

By this point I'd made considerable progress with my running and was feeling very confident. There were four or five factors that combined to make this possible. Reflecting back now, I can appreciate how it happened.

As we headed into the Massachusetts State Meet, I was coming off an undefeated cross-country season, setting six course records. I also won the All-Division Western Mass Cross-Country Meet, setting a course record. Heading into the state meet, I was mentioned as one of the favorites. How could I lose?

Right out of the gate, I failed to react quickly, and got off to a slow start. I ran like I was I in a fog, and was never able to make up that lost ground. The winner of the race was Charlie Maguire, whom I'd beaten soundly in a race the previous summer. I staggered in at *twenty-fifth place*, totally stunned at my epic loss.

Right after the state meet, it was announced that Pete Conway would become the new Greenfield High School track coach. This was the first time I had a coach who really understood distance running and training. Pete had been the captain of his cross-country team at the University of Massachusetts (UMass) and after graduating ran for the Boston Athletic Association (BAA). Pete competed in many road races and several marathons. In 1959, he won the National Twenty-Kilometer title for the Amateur Athletic Union (AAU) and was also a top finisher at the Yonkers Marathon. Pete coached the Greenfield High School cross-country team to a state championship in 1965. He was a wealth of knowledge and really knew how to make a plan to achieve goals.

Pete was friends with the UMass coach, Ken O'Brien. That January, he made arrangements for me to train indoors twice per week in Amherst with the UMass team. Curry Hicks Cage was a dusty field house with very dry air. There were heating units blasting out hot air on the turns. The wooden board track was firm in spots and very soft in others. Despite all that, I was psyched.

I'd never run indoors before, so it took a little getting used to. The UMass guys treated me like part of the team, and I even took turns leading some of the intervals with the freshmen. My motivation soared and my confidence grew. I was on the same track with Ron Wayne, Tom Derderian, and Tom Jasmine. Running in the Cage was also fun, as we were able to watch the basketball team practice while we did our workouts. Julius Erving, better known as Dr. J, who would become one of history's greatest NBA players, entertained us during our recovery jogs.

My first test was the state indoor meet at Boston Garden in February of 1970. Coach and Mrs. Conway brought me to the meet. The board track was eleven laps to the mile. Before the race I met Jock Semple, who was a trainer with the BAA. Pete ran for Jock in his BAA days. He told Coach Conway that he had a kid named Jim Kent who was going to run away with the high school two-mile race. Jock was right, Jim won, but I did manage to finish second.

Following the high school meet, we attended the BAA Games, which was one of the top indoor track meets on the circuit. We had the best seats, looking right down at the finish line. That night, I met John Thomas, an Olympian and former world record holder in the high jump. I saw Marty Liquori run the fastest indoor time in the world at that point in the season. Coach introduced me to many people who came up to greet him. I was overwhelmed.

During the winter, I learned that a transfer student named Rick Sherlund, from Baytown, Texas, would be joining our track team. I had to be prepared for this Sherlund guy; I heard he'd run a 4:29 mile as a freshman. I boosted my mileage to seventy-five miles per week. Coach had me doing lots of hill, running with exaggerated knee lifts for strength. I'd bound up the hill and do some brisk strides on the flat, then jog back down—and then repeat the whole thing three to ten times, depending on the hill.

In January, Rick Sherlund arrived. He was tall and lean with long hair held back with a headband. Coach told me to check out the new guy. Apparently, he'd seen Rick hitchhiking down Federal Street and cussing at the cars that didn't pick him up.

So I invited Rick to do a hill workout together. It was a freezing cold day, the headwinds were strong, and Rick had no hat or gloves. After the first few intervals, Rick huddled up between several large boulders and pulled his hands inside the sleeves of his sweatshirt, trying to keep warm, while I finished the workout. I felt bad for him, and as we jogged back to the high school I told him that the weather would get better over the next few weeks. He would soon prove himself to be a tough competitor.

At our first team meeting, Coach Conway announced that he would be holding mandatory Saturday morning practices at 9:30 a.m. There wasn't much grumbling about it, which showed that the team was really focused.

Rick and I became regular training partners and the best of friends. He started the season breaking the school record for the 880, while I broke the record for the mile. In the middle of the season, Coach moved Rick up to the mile and me into the two-mile. We only raced against each other one time. We faced off in a mile, which I won in 4:32.

Four days after our face-off, Rick broke my record for the mile, running 4:29. The same day, I broke my school record in the two-mile, clocking a 9:49. What amazes me about our times is they were both run on a rutted, uneven grass track. Every once in a while, I wonder how much faster we would have run on a modern track.

We trained at a very high level for high school kids. I didn't know any other Western Mass high school runners who were regularly training seventy miles a week. Our track workouts were tough and frequent. Here are two workouts from my running diary:

May 2:

    1½ miles in 7:25

    6 x 440 yards in 63.5 seconds

May 15:

    20 x 440 yards in 69 seconds

    5 x 220 yards in 31 seconds

We had a great group of athletes who were also really good guys. As teammates, we respected and supported each other. We made a commitment to be the best we could be, with our main goal to win the Western Massachusetts Championship. My personal goal was to win the state meet in the two-mile race.

Our first two meets set the tone for the whole season. We had decisive wins over Mohawk and Amherst. During those meets, our team set one school record and tied or just missed five others by a hair. It was obvious that we'd be tough in the distance events, with very strong milers and two-milers. Behind me was Rick Sherlund, Gary Burniske, Dave Thompson, Pete Wayman, and Steve Streeter. We had several multi-event athletes that continued to score big points all season long.

The true test of our strength was the following week, at the Steele Relays in Northampton. As the Springfield newspaper reported, "Greenfield stole the show." The distance medley was our key event. Rick Sherlund led off with a strong half-mile and handed off to Bill Cicia for a 220-yard leg. Chris Ryan ran a tough 440 yards and passed the baton to me for the mile anchor. I ran a personal record of 4:29 in the mile and we broke the event record by twelve seconds! Our 880 relay team also did well, finishing in first place.

Chris Ryan ended up scoring 136 points during the ten–dual-meet season. Chris had triple wins in six of the meets! I feel confident saying that this has never been duplicated. Chris was an excellent high jumper, low and high hurdler, quarter-miler, and relay runner. He set school records in all those events, ending up with a running total of six records. Near the end of the season, the newspaper wrote that an underclassman Steve Seredynski "could become the next all-around performer in the tradition that Chris Ryan had almost made legend."

We took some literary license informing Chris that he was now a legend and we began calling him "Legey." We meant it in a respectful way, but Chris hated it. He got even with me when he loosened the plumbing on the toilet in the locker room. When I flushed, water came gushing out on me like a fire hose! I don't think Chris knew how fast I could run as I chased him out the door and across the field. To this day, I have no idea what I would have done if I caught him. He would've crushed me. Chris was a lot of fun and had a lot of energy and still is a friend to this day.

Bill Cicia could also lay claim to "legend" status. Over my senior season, Bill scored 126 points for us. To this day, Bill's records in the 100- and 220-yard dash have never been broken. He was also the anchor of the record-setting 880-yard relay team. Bill acted as cheerleader for the distance runners, always yelling out, "Push it, every tenth of a second counts!" I remember him yelling this to our friend Paul Flannery of Cathedral during the Western Mass Championship mile race. Paul went by Bill and gave him a wave while smiling. Paul missed the meet record by one tenth of a second!

Our weight crew was also very strong. Jim Kaczenski set records in the discus and was a top javelin thrower. Ken Golosh was a big point-getter in the shot put and Mark Peters broke records in the triple jump and scored consistently in the long jump.

During the early spring, I received correspondence from many colleges, some even offering scholarships. But none of those schools excited me and most didn't offer my intended major, physical education. I put all my energies into my dream school, Springfield College. It was one of the top track programs in the country with a terrific coach, Vern Cox. It was also close to home, making it possible for my father to come watch me run.

At that point, life was good. I was running very well and I had a girlfriend, Sandy Misiun. Sandy was a sophomore whom I'd been seeing since February. She was smart, artistic, and very pretty. Sandy came to almost all of my meets to cheer me on. When I wasn't with Sandy, I hung with my friends Rick Sherlund and Pete Wayman. Everything seemed perfect—until I received the dreaded letter from Springfield College. "I am sorry to inform you..."

I was devastated. I'd put all my eggs in that one basket, and now I had no plan. To be fair to Springfield College, I was a terrible student. My grades were dismal and my college test scores were even worse. I felt like a dummy, a failure.

Much later in life, I learned about some of the underlying issues I had that were never diagnosed. In elementary school, I couldn't see the blackboard from my seat. I thought that was how everyone saw (or didn't see) the numbers in the front of the room. Because of that, I missed important foundational learning. In fourth grade, I had an eye exam and was told I needed glasses. When doing budget work in my first professional Y position, I noticed that the columns of numbers hardly ever added up correctly. What my colleagues would do in an hour would take me three or four. I later learned that I was dyslexic. Add a little attention deficit disorder to the mix and I began to understand: I wasn't a dummy after all.

On my own, I found a method to deal with all of these challenges. I rewrote my class notes and recorded myself talking through them, then listened to my recordings on the drive to school. The hard work eventually paid off, and in my senior year at the University of Massachusetts I was able to achieve all As and Bs. Later in my professional life, I was asked to be a keynote speaker at Springfield College Career Day. I found it ironic that the school that rejected me years ago had invited me to speak to their students on how to be successful in their careers.

Our distance runners worked hard and also had a lot of fun. One April Friday afternoon, Coach told us to go on a ten-mile run to the pumping station and back. In the past, this was our favorite loop, but vandals had burned down the historic covered bridge the previous Halloween, making it an out-and-back run. When we got to the bridge, we decided to run through the snow for a bit to see if there was a place we could cross the river and avoid retracing our course. The spring ice melt had the water pretty high and ice chunks flowed down the river at a fast speed. Even places where the river was normally low showed levels way over our heads. Finally, we thought we found a place to cross. Jim Dejoy took off his shoes and waded into the river. A third of the way across, the freezing cold water was up to Jim's chest.

We decided on Plan B. We began bushwhacking up the thickly forested hillside and finally came out on a road we knew. Pete Wayman recognized the house of a classmate, Gail Bellenoit. Pete instructed me to pretend I was injured and left us all in the driveway as he went up to ring the doorbell. Gail answered and Pete explained our (fabricated) situation. She reluctantly asked permission from her mother and we all loaded into her car. On the way back to the high school we saw Coach Conway's VW bus coming up the road. Of course, we all ducked down! We got back to the school, grabbed our stuff, and headed right home without bothering to shower or change.

I was only home a short time when the phone rang and my father said that Coach Conway wanted to speak to me. He said he saw our footprints going off into the snow and not returning. My feeble attempts to explain weren't accepted by Coach. He ended the call saying, "I'll see you at practice in the morning." When we arrived the next day, we noticed our workout was not posted on the bulletin board, as it usually was. We asked Coach Conway about that, and he said he had a special workout for us: 110-yard sprints. We had to do them until he told us to stop…which he didn't do until we'd done over twenty of them. Lesson learned (sort of).

In May, student protests against the war in Vietnam happened across the country. We talked about this during our Saturday morning workout. Rick and I did five repeat miles in 5:08 that morning. Coach told us to rest up on Sunday and get ready for a big week ahead. But we had other plans. We decided that as our protest of the war, we'd have a relay-style run to my aunt's home in Chicopee. We painted "Run For Peace" on a big plywood sign and tied it on top of Pete Wayman's 1965 Mustang. Then, off we went on our thirty-mile jaunt.

We traveled down Deerfield Street toward Amherst. Cars tooted their horns in support during the entire run. When we ran through the UMass campus, cheers and ovations erupted from a large student protest. Peace signs were flashed from the crowd as we ran through. We kept going, relay-style, until we reached our destination. We all felt good that we'd done something to promote the peace movement and our efforts didn't go unnoticed. Coach Conway and his wife were driving down Deerfield Street that morning and saw us running behind the Mustang with the Run for Peace sign!

Toward the end of the season, we had our annual meet with our archrivals, Turners Falls High School. This meet attracted many more spectators than usual. My close Turners Falls friend Michele Couture was there, along with her sister Karen. They tried to stay neutral, cheering for both teams. Through my friendship with Michele, several of our team members met and dated

Turners girls. It was a strong rivalry and this sometimes caused friction. We won the meet ninety-five to thirty-six!

The Western Mass Championship was held at the East Longmeadow High School. I remember it was a very hot, dry, and extremely windy day. Rick was second in the mile and I won the two-mile, setting the Western Mass record in 9:43. I was happy with my time, considering the conditions of the track. Being the last event of the day, the track was turned into a rutted dust bowl. I ran alone after the first lap and wasn't pushed.

At the state meet in the rain the following week, Coach told me two things: "Stay out of lane one," (it was so badly rutted up) and, "Don't get boxed in." For some reason, I failed to heed both: I found myself in the mud in lane one and got boxed in, unable to make a move. I ended up running the same time as in the Western Mass meet and finished sixth. Only the top four finishers qualified for the New Englands, which had been my goal all year long.

I was devastated that I didn't make the cut, sobbing on my girlfriend Sandy's shoulder, surrounded by my teammates. But I responded by doing what I'd always done after a defeat: I trained harder. I dedicated myself to running tough in summer road races. I decided to set my goal to run a twenty-four-hour relay and the first New York City Marathon.

Our 1970 track team was undefeated and went on to win the Western Massachusetts title. We averaged over a hundred points per meet, which is an amazing feat. All twenty-eight members of the team scored points during the season. All this was accomplished on a soft, rutted, uneven grass oval, with a first-year head coach, and a group of guys who had the desire to achieve.

Highlights of the 1970 Greenfield High School Track Team

- Fourteen school records set (many records broken multiple times)
- Undefeated dual-meet season
- Winners of the Steele Relays (two meet records)
- Western Massachusetts Champions AA (large-school category)
- One Western Massachusetts record (two-mile)

4

Holyoke Massacre

Running the Holyoke Marathon with no long training runs was probably not a good idea.

The longest training run I'd done during the track season was a thirteen-miler (a story all in itself). Holyoke was a tough course, starting and finishing on the midway at the Mountain Park amusement park. In addition to the course being especially hilly, the race was held at noon and finished in the heat of the day. And the course itself was totally exposed to the sun.

Starting at Mountain Park, the race was mostly downhill for the first six miles, followed by fourteen miles of city streets, and then the grinding six-mile climb back up to the finish. There were very few water stops and the roads were radiating heat. The finish line was located right on the midway, where we became another one of the park's amusements.

I remember those last six miles as particularly hot and painful. I quickly learned why they nicknamed the race the "Holyoke Massacre." My feet were blistered and I began getting muscle cramps. I was in survival mode.

I'd given my car keys to my friend Pete Wayman for safekeeping. Pete, Rick Sherlund, and Jim Dejoy, my support crew, thought it was a good idea to pick up some "refreshments" and drive the course to support and encourage me. They caught up with me with about four miles to go with no water, but obviously plenty of beer. I remember being angry with them for having a party while I was out there suffering, trying to survive and finish.

I forgave them shortly after finishing because an ice-cold electrolyte replacement drink is just what I needed to start my recovery process. I was beginning to get my sense of humor back until I asked where they got a cooler for all that beer. I soon discovered that they had improvised, making a cooler on the floor in the back seat of my car.

After Holyoke I took a few days off from running, then began a slow buildup of miles. I did a track workout five days after the race and had no physical problems. Soon, I was back up to sixty or seventy-five miles per week, including some speed work on the track. I trained with my buddy Frank McDonald, who was one of the people who encouraged me to go out for cross-country. Frank had just finished his freshman year at Providence College, where he ran cross-country and track. In the summer and during school vacations Frank was always there to keep me going, training and traveling together to road races.

During the summer of 1970, I continued to play a lot of tennis. I was always conflicted between running and tennis, which should take priority. I started out as a tennis player at a young age, traveling to tournaments and ranking in New England's twelve-and-under and fourteen-and-under brackets. In July I entered the county junior tournament, in which I'd been runner-up to Mark Fotopulos for nine years in a row. My fitness was at a very high level and I played my best tennis. I won, beating Mark for the first time: 6-3, 6-4.

I entered the men's tournament two weeks later and played Eduarda Gentil, a summer school student at Mt. Hermon School. Eduarda was the fifth-ranked junior in Brazil. I played a strong quarterfinal match but was beaten in two sets.

A week later, I teamed up with my long-time tennis coach Rich Kells and entered the men's doubles. We made it to the finals, where we played my old nemesis Mark Fotopulos and his partner Paul Chaput. We lost the match 6-3,6-4.

Getting to the finals wasn't easy. In the semifinals, we faced my father and his long-time partner Paul McDonald. Paul was a top tournament player with a very strong forehand and incredible quickness. A great athlete, Paul once won the Western Massachusetts high school tennis tournament as well as the Western Massachusetts high school mile in the same season. I'm not sure that his feat has ever been duplicated. Paul and my father had won the men's doubles title several times. That day, though, even though my father played solid tennis, Paul struggled. It was definitely an off night for Paul. We took advantage of this unusual occurrence and won the match 7-5, 6-1.

Our victory was bittersweet, as I didn't want to see my father lose the match—but still, I wanted to win!

It was time to get serious about running again. My buddy Frank saw an advertisement in *Runner's World* magazine for the third annual Grandfather Mountain Marathon, held in Boone, North Carolina. Frank told me the course record was 3:09. Since we'd both run much faster than that time, we thought about how cool it would be to travel down there and maybe win the race by tying each other. The race was advertised as being held in conjunction with the Highland Games and the last half mile was on a track in front of thousands of spectators.

We spent all the money we made as summer camp counselors at the Y and bought plane tickets from Hartford to Winston Salem, North Carolina. Several other runners picked us up at the airport and we began the long ride to Boone. It was during the car ride that we learned why the course record was 3:09. The guys in the car described the course as "beautiful, mountainous, and devastating." The elevation went up over a thousand feet total, then rose and fell repeatedly.

When we arrived in Boone, we drove the racecourse. Frank and I sat in the back seat, looking at each other with expressions on our faces that said *Holy crap*.

After a great meal at the Daniel Boone Inn, we came up with our strategy. We decided to start out at the back of the pack and see how it went. We'd run the first half together and then whoever felt better would pick up the pace. We conceded that we wouldn't be winning the race holding hands at the finish. We just wanted to survive.

The race didn't start till 11:00 a.m., which gave the temperature time to soar. Our strategy of starting at the back of the pack gave me a relaxed feeling and I started looking at the race as more of an adventure. Frank and I slowly worked our way up in the field and hit the half-marathon at 1:43:34. At this point Frank started to struggle, so I picked up the pace. I hit twenty miles in 2:40, and despite the hill-climbing, I felt tremendous. I ran the third-fastest last 10K in the field and finished in 3:26:10, good for sixteenth place. Frank struggled in at 4:28:03.

We went to retrieve our bags with our clothing and discovered that the vehicle carrying them to the finish had driven off a cliff! Fortunately no one was injured, and we eventually got our clothes back.

All in all, it was a great learning experience. We survived one of America's toughest marathons, although we didn't know that at the time. On our travel home we talked about our next adventure: running for twenty-four hours!

5

Twenty-Four-Hour Relay

My recovery from the Grandfather Mountain Marathon went incredibly quickly. I took one day off to travel home and the next day I drove to Forest Park in Springfield to run in the weekly Monday evening cross-country race. Forest Park and the surrounding area of East Longmeadow was a nice place to run. The cross-country course was a 2.3-mile loop with several hills. You ran around a field, on roads, and across dirt trails.

The king of Forest Park during the summer of 1970 was Mike Gallagher from Vermont, who attended graduate school at Springfield College. Mike was a great runner (four-time winner of the Mount Washington Race) but an even better cross-country skier. Mike competed in three Olympics and went on to coach the U.S. cross-country ski team.

Two days after Grandfather Mountain, I finished second to Mike at Forest Park. This became a pattern for the remainder of the summer: Mike winning and me coming in second. What made the Monday night races fun was the great competition followed by a social five- to seven-mile run with a great group of runners.

At the end of July, I received a postcard from my friend Ed Walkwitz. Ed was attending the Olympic training camp at Washington State University in Pullman, Washington. Ed wrote that some of the guys at the camp competed in a twenty-four-hour relay, on teams consisting of ten individuals, running a mile each in relay order for twenty-four straight hours. Ed said he "didn't have the guts to try it." He later said that he was glad he didn't, because the guys that ran were "really hurting…with Gerry Lindgren hurting the most." Gerry averaged 4:48 per mile for his thirty one-mile runs. It ranked him fifth among those who ran. Bill Scobey averaged 4:42 per mile!

With Ed opting out, I shared the postcard with my friend and running buddy, Frank McDonald. We did some research and discovered that if we could put together a team that averaged six minutes per mile for the course's 140 miles, we could be the best team on the East Coast. The rules were simple: ten runners on a team, running in the same order, one mile at a time, for twenty-four hours. If someone dropped out you couldn't replace them, which would make rest intervals even shorter.

We set our twenty-four-hour relay dates as September 2 and 3 and began recruiting our team. Our first recruit was my buddy Rick Sherlund. Rick, an outstanding miler, would help us keep average mile time down and help us get the record. Frank, Rick, and I began pulling together the rest of the team. Four current and former Greenfield High School runners were recruited: Dave and John Thompson, Jim Dejoy, and Gary Burniski. We needed three more to complete our team, so we asked runners from Turners Falls High School, our archrivals. Bob and John Pagoda and Mike Connelly were added to the roster. We named our team the Franklin County Runners.

Our high school coach, Pete Conway, agreed to be our head official. Pete helped us with the logistics and challenges as well as our goal strategy. We chose our high school track for the race location, because we figured the grass oval would be easy on the legs. There was no lighting at the track so we borrowed kerosene construction lanterns from the local Department of Public Works to place around the track, marking it. We set up a tent in the infield, complete with sleeping bags and coolers for water and juice.

On the day of the twenty-four-hour race, Coach Conway shot the starting gun at 8:00 a.m. I ran my first mile in 5:01, unsure how much energy to use. I realized right away that the hour in between each run was going to be a challenge. After you finish your mile, what should you do? Rest? Hydrate? Stretch? After what felt like a short period of time, your name was called, and it was time to run again.

I began averaging 4:53 per mile and thought, "Okay, this isn't so bad." Jim Dejoy finished a mile at midnight, putting the team at 167 miles. Thirty minutes later, I hit the wall, going from sub-five-minute miles to a 5:23. An hour later, we lost John Pogoda to fatigue. There was no way John could go on. Down to nine runners, our rest time was cut by six minutes and everyone was feeling the effects of the cold night, which seemed to penetrate our bodies. The warm day turned into an uncomfortable forty-two-degree night! The dampness of the evening air made everything wet. Many team members complained about difficulty breathing.

All through the night, we persevered. The on-deck runner would wake up the next runner, then off we went, aiming for the kerosene lanterns around the turns. The track became rutted and visibility was poor. We were hungry but didn't want to eat much because we'd be running again in less than an hour. Family, friends, and girlfriends stopped by throughout the night to bring snacks and refreshments and to offer encouragement.

Early in the morning, we lost our second runner. Dave Thompson was a whiter shade of pale and couldn't continue. Our rest time became even shorter. Then, the sun started to rise and so did our spirits. We were hungry, stiff, sore, and fatigued. Most of us didn't have more than a few short naps. I recalled Ed's postcard saying how bad the guys at the training camp were feeling. I now understood.

With two minutes and twenty-one seconds to go before the 8:00 a.m. finish time, it was my turn to run. With many people gathered to view the finish, I gave it all I had. I ran a 2:17 half-mile and squeezed in an extra 903 yards by the gun at 8:00. As a team, we totaled 241 miles and 903 yards, setting an East Coast record and ranking us thirteenth in the nation.

I averaged 5:13 per mile, running twenty-five miles in total. It was a brutal event, much harder than any marathon I'd run up to that point. This was a true test of physical and mental endurance. It would be a solid week before I recovered and started feeling normal again.

Despite my exhaustion, I knew that in eleven days there would be a marathon in New York City. That sounded interesting.

Now, whom could I talk into traveling to New York with me?

6

New York City Marathon

On Saturday, September 12, 1970, my buddy Rick Sherlund and I boarded the bus at Charon's Pharmacy in Greenfield. Our destination: New York City.

I'd seen an advertisement announcing "the first New York City Marathon" and I figured this might be the place to run a fast time. Rick had turned sixteen and had just started his junior year at Greenfield High School. I was eighteen and a freshman at Greenfield Community College. Neither Rick or I had been to New York City before, so this was a real adventure. I can't remember how I talked Rick into going. I might've said something like it'd be good to do longer runs to help him in his cross-country season! Rick was shaping up to be the top high school runner in Massachusetts that year.

The trip to New York was a long one. The bus seemed to stop at every city on the way. We couldn't afford the express bus ticket so ended up on the Metro Bus, which took five hours to get into the city. This gave us plenty of time to plan our arrival. We had no idea how to get to Central Park, where we would eat, or how to find the West Side YMCA. We hoped we'd be able to stay at the Y for the night. (Of course, we had no reservations.)

Exiting the Port Authority bus terminal, standing there amidst the tall buildings and crowded sidewalks of people who actually knew where they were going, we must have stood out like the rookies we were. We were a long way from Greenfield. We decided to walk from the bus station to the West Side Y on 63rd Street. When we checked into the Y, we found that we only had funds sufficient to cover a single room. We went up to our room, took the mattress off the bed, and placed it on the floor. Now we had two beds: one of us would sleep on the mattress and the other on the box spring.

At dinner time, we walked down 7th Avenue and found a Howard Johnson's. After a quick look at the menu, we ordered spaghetti and meatballs with lots of bread. When our waiter asked what we wanted to drink, I said, "We'll have a couple of Heinekens." A few minutes later, he returned with two beers for each of us! We looked at each other, shrugged our shoulders, and drank up.

After dinner, we decided to cut through Central Park to get back to the hotel. Another rookie move! I remember this guy asking us for a dollar. He showed us holes in his trouser pockets and told us he *could* kill us and take all of our money, but really, he just wanted a dollar.

We made fast tracks and headed back to our spartan accommodations at the Y.

When we awoke on Sunday morning, we went back to Howard Johnson's for pancakes. After eating our fill, we walked back to the Y to change into our running clothes and then down to the lobby to register. The Marathon entry fee was $1.00. It was predicted to be a hot day, with temperatures in the eighties. We made our way over to the starting line at the Tavern on the Green with 126 other runners.

The gun sounded at 11:00 a.m. and we were off. The course was one short loop followed by four big loops of the park. The race was promised to be traffic-free, which was true...apart from the thousands of walkers, bicyclists, rollerbladers, and skateboarders that we had to negotiate around. People seemed to be unaware that there was a marathon going on. I distinctly recall the smell of roasted chestnuts and the sound of steel drums as I made my way through the course.

I learned quickly that Central Park was a very hilly place. The 110th Street hill at the north end of the Park was a tough climb. I remember thinking that I had to do it three more times! There was only one water station that I remember. Between the heat and the hills, I was suffering. I kept moving, though, and finished thirteenth in 2:56 to the applause of about 150 spectators. Rick staggered in at 3:46, good for thirty-seventh place. Gary Muhrcke won the inaugural race, running 2:31:39. Tom Fleming finished second in 2:35:44.

At the awards ceremony, I received a plaque. The first ten runners were awarded commemorative watches. On a telephone pole was a beautiful handmade poster with the words "NYC Marathon" made with construction paper. I made off with it while Rick yelled out, "Look! Someone's stealing the sign!"

Because we were so sore and lame, we took the subway back to Port Authority. I distinctly remember walking down the subway stairs backward because our quads hurt so badly, we couldn't go forward. Once we made it down the stairs, we had that five-hour bus ride back to Greenfield to look forward to!

Reflecting back on the NYC Marathon, who knew that 126 runners in 1970 would turn into 50,000 runners in 2017...and that that $1 entry fee would rise to $295? The race course moved out of Central Park in 1976, stretching through all five boroughs, and becoming a major international event. The race date also moved to November. Tom Fleming and I became great friends and always had the 1970 NYC Marathon connection. Tom won two NYC Marathons, in 1973 and 1975.

Rick won the prestigious Catholic Memorial Cross Country Championship later in the fall of 1970. From NYC rookies on our first visit, Rick eventually became very comfortable in New York, becoming a partner at Goldman Sachs and was ranked as the #1 software analyst on Wall Street for seventeen years straight. In 1986 Rick was on the IPO team working with Bill Gates to take Microsoft public. Rick and I acted as Best Man at each other's weddings and remain lifelong friends.

The New York Road Runners Club officially honored the Class of 1970 on the twentieth Marathon anniversary in 1989. At the event, the 1970 finishers were invited to share their memories of that September day. When it came to Rick's turn to speak, he recalled crossing the finish line ahead of Tom Fleming, but Rick still had one more park loop to go! I shared how fortunate I felt to get on that bus in Greenfield that September morning and join 125 other runners to become a member of the Class of 1970.

7

They Called Me Coach

In the winter of 1976, I was a twenty-four-year-old part-time student at the University of Massachusetts in Amherst. I had classes in the mornings and I was looking for an afternoon job. My high school track coach, Pete Conway, recommended that I speak to Ralph Collins, who was the Athletic Director at Greenfield High School. They were looking to fill the position of head girls' track coach and Pete thought I'd have a shot at the job.

I called Ralph and spoke with him about the position. He seemed a little concerned with me being so young. However, the next day, Ralph called and told me I had the job! I was very excited and a bit nervous. The previous year I had coached the junior high school cross-country team, but I'd never coached track and field before. There were also several field events like the discus and javelin in which I had no experience at all. Pete assured me that he'd work with me and everything would turn out okay.

While registering for my spring classes at UMass, I added on a skills class, "Track and Field Coaching." The class was taught by UMass head coach Ken O'Brien. The class was perfect, just what

I needed as each event was broken down in detail and accompanied by coaching tips and drills. Coach O'Brien recommended a book, *Coaching Girls' Track and Field*, which I found excellent. I finally felt prepared for the challenge.

The third Monday in March, the first official day of high school spring sports, came quickly. Like most New England winters, this one seemed to linger. It was cold and windy and the "cow path"— the name given to the grass oval that served as the home track for the high school—was turning back and forth between ice and mud. Each spring, Pete Conway would go out on the field with measuring tape in hand and accurately create the markings and lanes. The cow path was muddy in the spring and by the end of the season there would be a rut worn into the surface. It wouldn't be till 2016 that Greenfield High School would finally have a real track.

I remember the first day of practice on that cold and windy Monday. About twenty-five girls showed up. I spoke to them about how I saw the pre-season going. I explained that being injury-free was one of the keys to a successful season. I told them our practices would focus on conditioning including strength training, aerobic conditioning, and flexibility. Because it was brutally cold and windy outside, we jogged our warm-up in the school hallways. From there, it was on to the universal exercise machine for strengthening and then to the mats in the lobby for stretching. Skills and drills would come next, including hurdles in the hallways.

It didn't take long to recognize that I had some very talented and energized athletes on the team. There were quite a few girls returning from the previous year. More than half of the team were juniors and seniors. Most of the sophomores were brand new to the sport, as there was no junior high school girls' track program at the time. Skills and conditioning progressed at a rapid pace, as we'd soon test ourselves against real competition. We seemed to have a well-balanced team and, with the exception of depth, I thought we'd be very competitive.

Our first meet of the season was against Mohawk Trail Regional. Mohawk had top performers, similar to us, but Mohawk had much more depth. We lost to them, but it was a close meet, which gave us confidence and motivated the team to work harder. We won our next five meets, setting us up for a rematch with the Mohawks at the Western Mass Championship.

During that 1976 season, many school records were set, including Patty Godzinski in the 100, Martha Finn in the 220, Hilary Knapp in the 440, and Jessie Ravage in the mile and two-mile. Carla Letourneau set a school javelin record and Anna Mathieu set one in the high jump. We were particularly strong in the relays, setting school records in the 440- and 880-yard events. The 440 relay team of Patty Godzinski, Ann Noga, Karen Decker, and Susan Galipault were top-ranked in Western Mass. Typically, most teams anchor with their fastest runner. Not us. We led off with our three fastest sprinters and I selected Susan Galipault to be our anchor. Susan had good speed, but more importantly, I knew if she were given a lead she would not relinquish it! Susan was a fighter and had a ton of guts. The strategy worked and the team finished unbeaten.

At the end of the season, we went to the Western Mass Championship, hoping to overtake Mohawk. It was a close, tough meet, which we lost to Mohawk by five points. Jessie Ravage set a new Western Mass record in the two-mile, running 12:08. Martha Finn set a new record in the 220 and Hilary Knapp ran a 60.2-second 440. Our relay team remained undefeated and our javelin thrower, Carla Letourneau, finished second. I told the girls they should be proud of their second-place performance and that we'd work harder next year and win the championship.

The 1977 season started out similar to the previous year, losing our dual meet to Mohawk. I really felt that we had a shot at winning the Western Mass title. I thought we had more top performers that could score big points in the championship meet.

The team worked extremely hard. The girls were in very good condition and we avoided any serious injuries, despite training hard. I remember one drill that involved fifty-yard sprints. I was a little perturbed that many of the girls weren't working as hard as they should that particular day. In my attempt to scold those who weren't performing, I directed attention to Patty and told the team that Patty always gives 100 percent. The next thing I heard was, "Coach, coach!" as the girls pointed behind me. Patty was lying on the grass, hyperventilating. She was fine after a few minutes, but I felt terrible.

On another occasion, we were on a bus trip to compete against Amherst High School. It was pouring rain and I heard the girls complaining about the weather. I told the team, "Amherst doesn't like to run in the rain—and we *love* to run in the rain. We're going to run in the rain and mud and beat them on their own track!" The girls began cheering, psyched and ready to go. We pulled into Amherst High School to find out that the meet had been canceled because of a flooded track!

On May 31 we gathered at Franklin County Technical High School in Turners Falls for the Western Massachusetts Championship. This was a great location, as they had installed the first synthetic track in the area. Back then, there were no divisions; all schools, big and small, were in the same competition. I had to admit, winning this meet was going to take some outstanding individual performances.

With five events to go, it was clear that we needed big points in all the remaining events to win. Patty Godzinski started us off, winning the 100, tying the Western Mass record of 11.8 seconds. The mile relay of Joanne Turner, Heidi Bates, Katie Knapp, and Hilary Knapp bested the field with a fast 4:12. Our undefeated 440 relay team of Patty Godzinski, Ann Noga, Jennifer Hyde, and Susan Galipault smoked the competition with textbook baton exchanges. Jessie Ravage won the two-mile, capping an undefeated season and setting a Western Mass record in 11:55. Jessie ran alone out in front, like she did in almost every meet. Contributing in big ways were Hilary Knapp's second-place finish in the 440 and Patty's third-place in the long jump. It was an amazing finish. We scored twenty-four of our thirty-one total points in the last five events!

I was so excited for the girls. They were presented with the Western Massachusetts Championship trophy and we all took a victory lap around the track. It was incredible to share the excitement and accomplishments that these young women achieved. I enjoyed two Western Mass track wins as an athlete myself, but this was the most special moment in my athletic career.

Over the three years I coached, I can recall most of the girls who were on the team. Most of them I haven't seen in forty years, which would make them fifty-seven to sixty years old now!

Katie Knapp was the first girl I coached as a junior high student. Somehow, I talked her into joining the boys' cross-country team. Katie now lives in Texas and is a grandmother. She's very active in fitness classes and fitness challenges. Jessie Ravage is a historical researcher and writer in Cooperstown, New York. I recently learned that Jessie has been coaching high school cross-country for twenty-seven years. It's a wonderful feeling when an athlete you coached goes on to be a coach themselves. I haven't talked to Ann Noga in many years, but I noticed her Facebook page is covered with running and triathlon pictures! Susan Galipault, who anchored that undefeated relay team, went on to become an assistant vice-chancellor at UMass in Amherst. She has a wonderful family and lives in Shelburne, Mass.

Although I haven't seen them in over forty years, I remember the girls' names and the events. Karen Decker, Mary O'Neil, Leslie Hayden, Beth Seibert, Nancy Jones, Colleen Ingraham, and Lynne Caouette, to name just a few. I was fortunate to have some very talented athletes. As my friend Tom Fleming used to say, "It's all about passion and desire to achieve. You can talk it up as a coach...but you can't coach it!" I was lucky to have coached a team that had a high level of passion and desire. I loved going to practice every day. It was a life-changing experience.

8

Hollywood

In 1981 I began running for the Greater Springfield Harriers. I knew Peter Stasz, the club president, from many years of running road races. Peter did a great job at organizing and promoting the GSH and he'd assembled a first-class team. Steve Snover was the top runner on the team. Steve was enjoying great success on the New England roads. Bob Neil, a former Holyoke Catholic High School and UMass standout, along with Mike Kelleher, Celio Hernandez, Garrett Mahoney, and myself, made up the team.

The National TAC Cross Country Championship was being held on November 29 in Burbank, California, and Peter wanted us to compete. We raised the funds by competing in several road races that offered prize money. I'm not sure how Peter came up with the balance for the trip, but plans were made and a men's and women's team were entered in the meet.

Peter planned to have the men's team fly out to California the day before Thanksgiving, with the women's team to follow on Black Friday. We gathered at Bradley Airport near Hartford,

Connecticut. Peter had everything organized and we boarded our flight. Once aboard the plane we saw a group from the Coastal Track Club, and I immediately recognized Paul Gorman, who was tearing up the New England roads. The flight was delayed, and once we finally started moving it felt like we were traveling on the tarmac forever. I remember Peter looking over at me and saying, "Seems like we're flying pretty close to the ground."

We landed in California and Peter went to pick up our rental car. We figured we'd only need to rent one car for our group, because Mike Kelleher's cousin was driving out from Western Massachusetts and would meet us at the airport. Our biggest concern was getting to the hotel and getting in a run before dark. The pre-holiday crowds caused a delay in getting our rental car and Mike's cousin had not yet arrived. Paul decided that the parking garage was as good a place as any to get his run in. Wearing his jeans and sweatshirt, he took off and ran five miles, doing loops in the garage.

Finally Peter drove up in the rental car and we waited for Mike's cousin to arrive. A few minutes later, a beat-up old pickup truck pulled in, with a blue tarp covering the truck bed. Mike exclaimed, "Cousin Gene is here!" A bearded Cousin Gene, along with his truck, looked like he just arrived from the hills of West Virginia. Some of us got into the rental car with Peter and the overflow traveled in the bed of the truck under the tarp with Cousin Gene. The Harriers had arrived in Hollywood!

We received our first lesson on LA rush-hour traffic. It was unbelievable! It took almost two hours to go a relatively short distance to our hotel. It was total gridlock. We could have walked faster. We finally arrived at our hotel, which was—and I kid you not—the Hotel California! Peter selected the hotel because it was the race headquarters, close to the site of the race, and we received a discount. I was thinking of the lyrics of the Eagles song, *Hotel California*. This was far from a lovely place; it was a dingy hotel at best. As Peter surveyed the lobby, complete with five-gallon buckets to catch the water from the leaky ceiling, the first thing he said was, "The women can't stay here."

We got ourselves checked into our rooms. To save money, we were paired up with a roommate. I bunked with a member of the Coastal Club, John Forester. We changed up and headed out into the darkness for an hour-long run. After the long day, it felt really good to stretch and get our legs moving. During the run, we had to keep crossing busy streets. At one point, we'd stopped on a curb, chatting, when I stepped onto the road. Immediately Bob Neil grabbed me and pulled me back. A car sped by, missing me by inches. I could feel the breeze from the car. For the rest of our run, I was shaking in my shoes. That was the closest call I've ever had.

On Thanksgiving, Peter made reservations for us to have a turkey dinner at the Hilltop restaurant. The Hilltop was located in the middle of the DeBell golf course, the site of the meet. DeBell was a beautiful hilly course carved into a canyon. The restaurant was a great location, as we could view the racecourse, which was being closely guarded, allowing no runners on it. I remember thinking how strange it was to be sitting across the country in a Burbank restaurant having Thanksgiving dinner away from family.

On Friday, the day before the race, we went up to the second floor to register and pick up our race packets. The registration tables had long lines, as they didn't have enough help. I jumped behind the table and took charge of handing out the race T-shirts. The shirts were beautiful, yellow with green graphics. Some of the shirts accidentally slipped into my running bag, providing me with Christmas presents for my family and friends back home!

While we were at the registration, Peter scurried around to find acceptable accommodations for the women's team. When they arrived, Peter checked them into a nice Marriott hotel.

Besides going out for runs and eating meals together, there wasn't much to do. Bob Neil discovered that there was a marathon series of *The Twilight Zone* on television. In some ways, between the hotel, Cousin Gene, and being away during Thanksgiving, it felt like we were in *The Twilight Zone*!

The morning of the race, the men's team arrived in the pickup truck with Cousin Gene while Peter picked up the women's team in the rental car. I'll never forget the look on people's faces when we began climbing out of the tarp-covered bed of the pickup truck. I heard one guy say, "You've got to be kidding me."

The golf course at the scenic DeBell Country Club was saturated with water. It hadn't rained in southern California for several months—and then, three days before the race, a soaking rain arrived and lasted a full forty-eight hours. The golf course was a sponge, soaking up all the water that was dumped on it. A drought, and then a monsoon—what were the chances?

The gun went off and some of the who's who of distance running charged to the front. I remember seeing Alberto Salazar, Steve Scott, Henry Rono, and Nick Rose in the lead group. We tore up the course pretty badly. Mud flew everywhere. Several times I thought my shoe was going to come off and get stuck in the mud. The course was very tough with many hills.

Adrian Royal, a relatively unknown runner from England, won the race. Adrian ran at a world's-best pace, beating Salazar to the finish. The winning time was 27:20! Steve finished strong in 30:08 and I ran a 32:05 on the challenging 9,800-meter course. I remember standing around with the team after the race, all of us covered in mud from head to toe. The golf course was badly damaged and would require extensive work.

After the race, we piled into the rental car and Cousin Gene's truck to head back to the hotel. Once we showered off all the mud, we went to Hollywood. Peter secured tickets to *The Tonight Show* starring Johnny Carson. It was so much fun. At home, I watched Johnny's monologue almost every night. Buddy Hackett was the main guest the day we attended, and he was hilarious.

Returning to the hotel, we celebrated with dinner and drinks. I retired to my room exhausted and fell fast asleep. I was awakened at one in the morning by my roommate, who thought it was a great idea to bring some of his newfound lady friends from the bar back to our room. I was fuming, but trying to talk sense into this group of drunk strangers was a waste of time. Half in a fog, I got myself dressed and went to the lobby, taking all my things with me, afraid of getting ripped off. After spending an hour trying to sleep on the couch in the lobby, the guy working the desk felt sorry for me and found me a vacant room so I could get a few hours of sleep.

I kept thinking about that Eagles song, "Welcome to the hotel California, what a lovely place…" Not!

9

São Paulo Dream

Back in the late sixties, one of the challenges of being a runner was getting good information about running. How should you train? How do others train? Where do you find races?

To get answers, I subscribed to the magazine *Distance Running News*, which later became *The Runner's World* and then *Runner's World*. It was in a 1970 issue of *Runner's World* that I read about the São Silvestre New Year's Eve race in São Paulo, Brazil. This race attracted great runners from all over the world, and it captured my imagination instantly. Imagine running a race and finishing at midnight, in a new year, in South America! *Someday*, I thought, *I'll run this race!*

Fast forward a good decade and a half.

In 1987, Bill Rodgers and I were training together almost every day. It helped that I was now living just a few miles away, in Natick, Mass. Bill would come over to my place to start one day, and I would go to his the next.

Our typical afternoon run was six to ten miles, and it was on one of these runs that Bill mentioned he was going to a race, and that he had an extra plane fare with accommodations if I wanted to go with him. That race? São Silvestre.

After all those years, it was really going to happen!

Traveling with Bill has always been an interesting adventure. Bill has a reputation for cutting it close, time-wise. We arrived for our flight to Brazil in the nick of time; they were getting ready to close the plane door. We were so late, they'd given away our coach seats. Luckily, the gate agent recognized Bill, and a few minutes later we found ourselves sitting in first class!

After the long flight to Brazil, we arrived in Rio and took a connecting flight to São Paulo. I asked Bill some basic questions like, "Who's picking us up? Where are we meeting this person? Do you know them?" Bill didn't have any answers, but he seemed pretty relaxed, so I decided to go with the flow.

We were met at the airport by a Colombian running agent named Carlos, who brought us to our hotel. Along the way, I remember seeing unbelievable poverty and felt shocked and saddened by the deplorable conditions people lived in.

Finally we arrived at our hotel, which also served as the race headquarters. The first thing we saw was a long line, reaching nearly around the entire hotel, of runners waiting to pick up their race numbers. When we exited the car, runners abandoned their places in line, swarming Bill and asking for his autograph. Someone told me that many things in Brazil, including athletics, were as much as ten years behind the U.S. Suddenly it was 1979 again and Bill Rodgers was king!

We checked into our hotel room, which was near the top of the building. Our room had four single beds and what Bill called a "refrigo-bar." Bill remembers the race official saying we could help ourselves to it; I recall the opposite. In any case, we had the refrigo-bar restocked three times during our stay, eating all the snacks and drinking the tasty Antarctica beer. When we departed, we didn't take any chances and did a very quick checkout.

I attended the pre-race press conferences and TV promotions with Bill. I even signed autographs myself; some people thought I must be a famous Italian/American runner. São Paulo has the second-largest Italian population outside of Italy. The night before the race, they brought us to the tallest building in São Paulo. It was named after an Italian and from the observatory, you could see the whole race course. The news media exited the elevator but instructed Bill and me to stay on. They closed the doors and then reopened them so they could film us walking out onto the observation deck for the first time.

The next day, Carlos brought us to a park to run. As our group was enjoying the run on the road, a Jeep carrying four soldiers with big automatic weapons drove up beside us. Carlos and the soldiers began a heated conversation in Spanish. Bill and I had no idea what was being said when suddenly Carlos shouted to us, "Corre, rápido!" and the group began sprinting across a field. When the coast was clear, I asked Carlos what was going on and he told me the soldiers said to get off the road, the roads were not for running. Apparently, Carlos told them where they could stick their rifles.

The rest of the run was uneventful, thank God. There was a film crew in the park waiting for us to run by. I recognized the crew from the night before and gave them a wave. Bill scolded me, saying that I was a rookie waving to the press. That night we were watching the news and there came our group across the field, with me waving at the camera. Bill just shook his head and repeated, "Rookie!" I remember thinking how strange it was seeing yourself on TV at night and not understanding a thing they were talking about, since it was all in Portuguese.

Bill brought a pocket full of Brazilian currency, left over from a previous trip when he ran the Rio de Janeiro Marathon. We soon found out that the government had changed currency some years before and his wad of money was now worthless. We ended up tossing it out the hotel window, watching as the air current floated the money high into the sky!

Down below in the streets, people had started their New Year's celebrations. It was very festive, to say the least. Brazilian people really know how to party. By mid-afternoon, businesses (with the exception of bars) began closing down. People started gathering in outdoor cafes. We kept hearing loud firecracker noises down in the street. We noticed that every few minutes, someone would run out of a building and shoot a gun up in the air. A real gun!

On the evening of the race, we piled into a VW Fox and headed for the race starting line. One guy in the car was excited to learn I was from Boston. He loved the Celtics and he knew all the players' names and statistics. His name was José Luiz Barbosa. José went on to win the World Indoor Track Championship the following year and took silver and bronze at the outdoor World Championships four years after that. He had a 1:43.08 800-meter best.

At the starting line there was a huge party, with thousands of people yelling, blowing horns, and drinking. It was obvious that some in the crowd would be jumping into the race, fueled by the day-long party. The race started at 11:00 p.m. Despite the late hour, it was wicked hot and very humid! Bill and I started out together on the 7.8-mile course. We clicked off three five-minute miles and I was feeling pretty good. By mile four, Bill picked up the pace and I began to struggle a bit.

Spectators constantly threw firecrackers into the road, which added to the challenge. The course was mostly dark, with the exception of the major intersections. At those spots, it was like daylight, with bright lights and television cameras all around. I remember people advising me not to drink the water so I didn't. Not a drop. Approaching the finish line, I was doing the weave! I knew I was in tough shape, totally dehydrated, and really struggling. As I finished the race, a massive fireworks display went off close by. Residue from the fireworks rained down on me so I ducked under a tin-roof pavilion. It sounded like hailstones hitting the metal of the roof.

I finally found Bill signing autographs and actually giving a guy the shirt off his back. I told him I was badly dehydrated, felt terrible, and needed to get back to the hotel. The last thing I wanted was to end up in a São Paulo hospital.

Once back at the hotel, I tried to get my body temperature up by taking a hot shower, but I couldn't stand up. I crawled into bed and Bill placed all the blankets from our room's four beds on top of me. And I drank everything in the refrigerator bar! I had to cup my hand over the glass bottle opening so I wouldn't chip my chattering teeth. I eventually fell asleep with my body shivering violently. Classic hypothermia.

The next morning, I awoke feeling fine, as if it had never happened. It was an amazing recovery. We went to the park near the hotel and ran five miles, doing one-mile loops, with a group including Dave Murphy from England. We all met for a group breakfast and then headed to the airport. It was a whirlwind trip, with some unforgettable memories. Most importantly, I had finally participated in the race that I had dreamed of as a young high school runner sixteen years earlier.

Photos

Me and my father at the 1970 Western Mass track Meet in East Longmeadow.

1970 Undefeated Greenfield High School "Dream Team."

Setting a school track record (9:49) on the "cow path."

Boxed in during the 1970 State Championship 2-mile race.

Training with my teammates L to R: me, Rick Sherlund, Jim Dejoy, Dave Thompson, and Gary Burniske.

Pete Wayman's message in my high school yearbook. They were still searching for whoever really burned the covered bridge down!

A bit embarrassing walking into school every day.

"Out of the Mystic" Winning a race for the Mt. Park Athletic Association.

The start of the first New York City Marathon, 1970.

A 1970's trip to Bloomfield NJ to visit my friend Tom Fleming.

L to R: me, Chris Ryan, and Frank McDonald celebrating after an indoor meet at UMass.

SOMEWHERE, SOMEONE IN THE WORLD IS TRAINING WHEN YOU ARE NOT. WHEN YOU RACE HIM, HE WILL WIN.

— *Tom Fleming* —

Tom Fleming's mantra.

Frank McDonald and me at the finish of the Mt. Washington Road Race.

Playing in the Franklin County Junior Tennis Finals.

L to R: Mike Kelleher, me, and Denny Tetreault showing off our winning prizes after the Agawam road race.

L to R: Marty Flynn, me, Connie Putnam, Mickey Campaniello, Denny Tetreault, Jeff Lamoureaux, and Ed Porter preparing for a New Year's Day long run.

Battling it out with Jack Mahurin in the WAQY road race in Springfield.

TV interview after placing third in the WAQY road race for the second year in a row.

Finishing a ten-mile run with Ken Kaczenski on the river road in Greenfield.

L to R: My brother Greg, me, Mickey Campaniello, and Jim Allen after the Josh Billings Triathlon in Lenox MA.

Denny Tetreault and me at the start of the Easthampton MA road race.

Bill Rodgers and me at the BAA Mayor's Reception in Boston.

Bill Rodgers and me running the Faneuil Hall road race.

Running the banks on the Harvard indoor-track New England 3,000-meter championship.

L to R: Bill Rodgers, Tom Fleming, and me celebrating St. Patrick's Day in Boston.

L to R: Pete Conway, me, and Chris Ryan having a reunion.

L to R: Rick Sherlund, Coach Conway, and me at the dedication of the Greenfield High School's new track, the Peter Conway Memorial Track.

Me and Don Clark, my friend and boss when I worked at Clark's Sport Shop in Greenfield.

L to R: me, Jim Allen, and Frank McDonald at the Greenfield Y Road Race.

Jon Barnes and me at the Boston Marathon.

My friend Jamie O'Neil playing a few tunes at his home in Kingston MA.

Rick Sherlund and me on the rooftop of Rick's home on Nantucket.

Sailing my boat *Sundance*.

A lifetime of running and friendship, Tom Derderian and me.

L to R: Fred Doyle, Bob Hodge, me, Bill Rodgers, and Jon Barnes at our annual New Year's Day open house.

My first mate Ginger and me.

10

Cemetery

In the late seventies, I often drove down to Springfield College to meet up with my buddy, Jack Mahurin, Ph.D. Jack was the exercise physiologist on the faculty at the college. Along with being one of the leading authorities in the field of exercise science, Jack, a southern transplant who ran for the North Carolina Track Club, was an outstanding runner. Jack won the second annual Cherry Blossom ten-mile race in Washington, D.C., and finished twelfth in the Boston Marathon, running a 2:23. I met Jack when he came to Greenfield and won the Y road race, pushing me back to third place.

Jack was responsible for developing a curriculum that prepared students to work as fitness professionals in the Y. He recruited Jim Allen from our Greenfield Y as part of his task force. Jim was my mentor at the Y and was a wealth of practical knowledge on exercise science. Amazingly, Jim had no college degree and was self-taught. He constantly read and attended conferences. I was with Jim at a conference when he raised his hand and asked a question of the speaker. The gentleman responded to

Jim, "That's an excellent question, sir. Are you a doctor?" From then on, we called Jim "Doctor Allen."

Jack invited me down to Springfield to run one of his Wednesday afternoon "quality workouts." I wasn't sure what they were all about, but I figured it would help with my training. I arrived at Jack's office, which was housed in a very old building at the entrance to the campus. After changing into our running clothes, we jogged up Alden Street about a mile and a half and turned into the entrance of Saint Michael's Cemetery, of all places.

Jack told me that his "quality workouts" were designed to simulate New England road-racing conditions. He reasoned, "Why would you run on a smooth track when road races are on hard surfaces with lots of sharp turns?" It made perfect sense. The cemetery provided the ideal environment. That day we ran five one-kilometer repeats before jogging back to campus.

I continued to train with Jack once a week. Most of the time, the "quality workouts" were in the cemetery, but we also ran in Forest Park. I felt myself getting stronger, with my mileage building in those the once-a-week sessions with Jack. We ran everything from 400s to repeat miles, all faster than race pace with a fairly short recovery period.

In April, I ran against Jack in the WAQY radio station Springfield road race. This was a five-mile race, the largest of its kind in Western Mass, and about a thousand runners entered. Dan Dillon and Bob Hodge showed up, so it looked like first and second place were taken.

We went out pretty hard and Jack and I were neck-and-neck as we ran up a steep hill at the two-and-a-half-mile mark. There was a big crowd and the road narrowed. The theme tune from *Rocky* blared from giant speakers from the radio station. The music gave me goosebumps and I surged ahead of Jack.

It was a two-man race between Jack and me, as Dan and Bob separated from us right from the start. I could feel Jack on my shoulder, trying to maintain contact. We flew down Main Street, streaking toward the finish line. The theme from *Chariots of Fire* blared from the many speakers that were set up. It was a really thrilling moment. I held Jack off and finished third, with him right behind me in fourth. We jogged to the beer tent, with Jack joking that we were the first ones to get a brew. Jack called home to his wife Suzy and admitted that I'd beaten him; however, he told her, "The sun was casting a glare off Joe's bald head and I couldn't see the finish line!"

My friend Mickey Campaniello later became Jack's teaching assistant at Springfield. It was fun seeing Mickey on my visits to the campus. He told me that Jack was an incredibly tough professor. Mickey told him once that a particular exam was too hard and Jack replied, "Either they know the material or they don't!"

One night after a workout, Jack and Suzy invited us to their house for a barbecue. Jack had this large, beautiful globe in the living room. Mickey and I were admiring it when Jack demonstrated its other use, opening the globe and revealing a huge collection of liquor. Jack pulled out a bottle of moonshine that his brother made and passed it around. The next thing we knew, Jack went upstairs and came back down playing the bagpipes! (Susie, who had gone to bed, was not amused.)

I took Jack's cemetery idea back to Greenfield and wheel-measured a local graveyard, marking it out in increments from a quarter-mile up to a mile. I painted the measured markers on the road in red paint. Ironically, the half-mile mark was right in front of my family's burial plot. The cemetery was a mile from the Y, which was a good warm-up distance.

My first workout at the cemetery was with Ken Kaczenski. We jogged up to the cemetery from the Y, carrying our racing shoes in our hands. We ran five 1Ks, each in 2:58, with a short jog in between. We tried to keep all our intervals below race pace. The shorter the interval, the faster the pace. The next week we ran four quarter-miles in seventy seconds, one mile in 4:48, then four quarter-miles in seventy seconds. The sharp turns and hard top roads did indeed simulate road racing conditions.

Over the next few months, our cemetery group grew to about a dozen. Some of our Y joggers became interested in what we were doing on Wednesday afternoons. Soon I was planning workouts for many of them. We all jogged together to the cemetery, did our workouts at our own paces, then jogged back to the Y. It became a weekly event on our training schedules. It was the perfect place to run, traffic-free and very quiet.

Jack eventually left Springfield and enrolled in the University of New England Medical School in Maine. He added a Doctor of Osteopathic Medicine in Exercise Physiology to his Ph.D. Jack returned to his southern roots and now serves on the medical staff of a Montgomery, Alabama, hospital emergency room.

11

Polish Picnic

One of the most fun activities of the summer was the Polish picnic on Sunday afternoons. The weekly event was held in the Greenfield Meadows. The picnic grounds had a large parking lot and covered pavilion, bordered by the beautiful green river. Cheeseburgers with fresh onions and a cold beer were on the menu. You could spend the afternoon enjoying the food and the live Polish music while catching up with friends.

Back in the late 1970s, I wanted to organize an annual Thanksgiving race and immediately thought the Polish picnic grounds would be the perfect place. The location was just right. I wheel-measured the course, which was 4.2 miles. It was a fast course, mostly flat with the exception of one hill.

Several years later, I lengthened the course to 4.7 miles by adding a figure-eight loop. It was a fun course for spectators, as the 2.6-mile mark passed right by the starting/finish line.

We had a small race planning group, which included Mickey Campaniello, Ed Porter, and several other Poet Seat Ridge

Runners. One of our committee members knew the owner of a local turkey farm and arranged for turkeys to be donated as prizes for the top male and female finishers in the open and masters categories. Someone thought it'd be a great idea to offer the winners a choice of either a live turkey or a frozen turkey. Sure enough, the turkey farm delivered the frozen turkeys along with one live turkey in a large kennel, complete with a collar and leash! To promote the race, Mickey and I decided to walk the turkey down Main Street to Clark's Sport Shop. Needless to say, the turkey drew lots of attention. The local newspaper sent a photographer to take a picture of us and the turkey, with Mickey holding a small hatchet someone handed him. The next day, we were on the front page of the newspaper. The Turkey Trot race was on the map.

I won the first Turkey Trot and selected the frozen turkey.

The race was a great success and would continue for the next eight years. The 4.7-mile course was so popular that we began to have monthly races there. The Thursday night runs included elite runners as well as recreational joggers. Many times, we had over fifty participants.

In 1983, I came up with a few new ideas to add a little more interest to the Thursday night races. The first event was the Snowball Classic, with teams of four people. The first runner would race to the mile mark, tag the second teammate, and they'd run together to the two-mile mark. There, they'd tag the third teammate and run together to the three-mile mark, where their final teammate was waiting. Then, the team of four runners would run to the finish. To win, the team had to cross the finish line together. It was a big hit and we had over twenty teams. It was fun and required strategy, as you could only go as fast as your slowest runner.

Later that August we held our second specialty race, The Twosome. Similar to the Snowball Classic, the first team member would run to the 2.6-mile mark, tag their partner, and the twosome would run together for the last 2.1 miles to the finish. Like the Snowball, the pair had to come across the finish line together to win.

People scurried around, trying to put together a winning team. Three weeks before The Twosome, I was in North Carolina, running in the Maggie Valley Moonlight Run. A friend of mine, Nancy Conz from Easthampton, was one of the elite seeded runners there. Nancy won the Ottawa and Chicago Marathons and was really tearing up the roads. I asked Nancy if she would be my partner in The Twosome and she said, "Of course!"

I ran the first 2.6 miles under a five-minute pace. I tagged Nancy and off we went together. I was fatigued but Nancy kept pushing the pace and I didn't want to let her down. Nancy dragged me in the last mile and we crossed the finish line together, winning the race.

Over the years, I lost touch with Nancy. Then, in 2016, we reconnected on Facebook and renewed our friendship. In February of 2017, Nancy passed away from cancer at age fifty-nine. I always enjoyed her company and remember going for training runs and having dinner with Nancy and her husband, Paul. Nancy was down-to-earth and very unassuming; a real classy lady. I am so grateful that we had the chance to reconnect once more.

12

The Rookie

During the winter of 1982, I was training hard and consistently, aiming for a successful spring and summer road race season. The winter was a tough one for Western Massachusetts—cold, windy, and more ice than snow. To top it off, most of my training runs happened after work, at 6:00 p.m., in the darkness.

I was beginning my semester of student teaching as a physical education major at UMass, Amherst. I was finally going to graduate after quite a few starts and stops. I definitely took the long and winding road. The standing joke in my family was, *Will Joe graduate before he turns thirty?* I made it—by forty-five days.

My student teaching assignment was elementary physical education in the Greenfield school system. This was perfect for me, teaching in my hometown. Even better, my high school track coach would be my supervisor! Working with Coach Conway was an incredible experience. He took creativity in the classroom to a whole new level. Most of the schools had no gymnasiums, leaving the classroom or cafeteria as the P.E. setting. To top it off, the only equipment we had was a cardboard box with items like bean bags, nerf balls, and a parachute inside. We were inventive with our new game activities. Marching to Village People tunes was a personal favorite of the space-confined program.

Five days a week, we traveled to all the elementary schools in town, bringing the cardboard box with us. We taught the kids cooperation, as the first activity was moving all the desks and chairs to the sides of the classroom. If we made too much noise, the principal would come and ask us to be quiet; not your typical gym class environment. My experience was very different than most of my classmates'. Most worked in gymnasiums and had ample equipment and supplies.

Coach Conway gave me a tremendous teaching experience, treating me as his co-teacher, sharing the planning and teaching of the classes. During the middle of the semester, Coach had knee surgery. (He was attempting an 11′6″ pole vault and injured himself.) I'm not sure how he did it, but Coach got approval for me to continue on my own for several weeks, getting paid as a substitute teacher.

When school finished, I would hurry on down to Main Street to work at Clark's Sport Shop. When I decided to go back to school in the late seventies, I was working full-time at Clark's, and Don Clark asked me to continue on a part-time basis while I was in school. Don was one of my biggest supporters through the years. He would put my worn shoes in his window display, attaching a sign saying, "Joe Martino ran 865 miles in these shoes." Don was always so accommodating, allowing me time off to run important road races. He even sponsored me to compete in the Schlitz Lite National Championship in Tampa, Florida.

In January, Coach Conway told me he had a runner whom he'd recruited from the soccer team. He told me, "The kid has great potential," but needed to get stronger. He asked if he could accompany me on my 6:00 p.m. training runs. His name was Ken Kaczenski. I knew two of Ken's older brothers: John, who was a top runner on the Greenfield High School cross-country team in 1964, and Jim, who was a teammate and friend of mine. Jim was an outstanding discus thrower and also a star on the basketball and football teams.

I called and invited Ken on my training runs, telling him we'd leave my house at 6:00 p.m. sharp.

On Monday evening, January eleventh, the temperature was zero degrees Fahrenheit and the roads were very icy. Denny Tetreault, my training partner, arrived at my home and we decided to run the Country Club Road ten-mile loop. We planned to run by Carry Crossman's house along the way so he could join us. Ken arrived just before six and we headed out into the elements. Dressed in our reflective vests and carrying our disposable plastic flashlights, we were ready. I remember Ken struggling at first. He was a pretty quiet guy, but we could tell the pace was clearly taxing him. He seemed to enjoy listening to our conversation about training, taking it all in. We nicknamed Ken "the Rookie." We finished the run in sixty-eight minutes, with ice hanging from our hats. I wondered if Ken would be back.

Sure enough, the Rookie showed up the next night, and the next. In fact, he hardly missed a night the rest of that winter. Denny Tetreault was always there and others drifted in and out. Carry, Roger Reid, Ed Porter, and Connie Putnam all made regular appearances.

As the weeks went by, Ken grew stronger and stronger. He began to speak up more and often pushed the pace. We averaged seventy-seven miles per week through the wicked winter weather. In February, we decided it was time to test our fitness and entered the Amherst ten-mile road race.

In that race, I went out with the leaders and passed two miles in 9:58. I made it through the icy reservoir stretch very slowly and carefully, losing contact with the top runners. I was deathly afraid of falling on the ice. I remember running at full speed down the hill to the finish, making the sharp turn into the final stretch, then looking back and seeing Ken twenty seconds behind me! I was pleased with my eighth-place finish in 52:58 and was stunned with Ken's performance.

At the end of March, I asked Ken to run a three-mile race with me. The plan was to run 4:58 per mile and Ken agreed to give it a try. We finished together in 14:54, right on pace. The following week was the national 10K championship in Boston. The day of the race was cold and windy. I went out hard, hitting the mile in 4:48, the two in 9:52, and three in 14:52. As we made the turn with three miles to go, I was running out of gas. I looked at the runners making the switchback and I saw that Ken was five seconds behind me. I pushed with everything I had to the finish line ahead of Ken, by three seconds!

We went to the Union Oyster House for a post-race dinner. We were celebrating as our team, the Greater Springfield Harriers, took the bronze medal. Ken looked at the menu like it was written in a foreign language. He ordered "garlic bread, without the garlic." It was then I realized he had never eaten in an upscale restaurant before.

In fact, Ken had very limited experience outside of Greenfield. That national 10K was his first trip to Boston. Ken's father died when he was just one year old. His mother, Annie, raised six children, five boys and one girl, all on her own. In addition to John and Jim, Ken's brother David was the high school javelin record-holder, and Ken's twin brother Keith was a very good athlete, too. Ken's sister Ann went on to work for the local probation department.

On April 25, we ran in the WAQY road race in Springfield. At the time, it was the largest race in Western Mass. It was as if summer had just appeared overnight, with temperatures suddenly soaring into the mid-eighties. I ran a tough race and finished third, with the Rookie right behind me in fourth.

That would be the last time I would ever finish ahead of Ken.

The winter training in 1982 paid off. Ken went on to run a 9:09 two-mile and rank as one of the top high school runners in the nation. After graduation, Ken spent a year at Greenfield Community College and began winning road races wherever he ran. Northeastern University offered Ken a full scholarship and off he went to Boston the following fall. Ken excelled at track and cross-country, achieving All-American status. He was excellent in all long distances but was especially outstanding at the steeplechase. Ken graduated in 1988 with a degree in economics and went to work in banking.

At that time, I'd moved to Newton, and Ken was living in Brighton right down the road, in a household of top post-collegiate runners. Among them were Brad Schlapak, who went on to win the National TAC Cross Country Championship, and Tim Gannon, who was also a first-class runner. Needless to say, it was a very competitive household. My wife Ginger and I lived at the one-mile mark of Ken's Heartbreak Hill loop. He would call me on the phone and tell me when they were leaving for a run and I'd wait outside to join in. I got a kick out of the situation; it was as if life had come full circle. I was now the one who was too winded to talk as I struggled up Heartbreak Hill each night with this group of running studs!

In 1995 Ken won the Fairhaven Father's Day road race. After the race, Ken took off his running shoes and gave up running. He told me he didn't have the drive to compete anymore. He was still disappointed he didn't qualify for the Olympic trials in 1992. Ken and I drifted out of communication, though I tried to connect with him many times over the next few years. In 2002, Coach Conway was inducted into the Massachusetts Track Coaches Hall of Fame. Ken attended the event with me and spent the night at our house. He soon drifted away again.

The next time I connected with Ken, he was working in auto financing at a VW dealership in Northampton. I drove up and took him to lunch and we reminisced about old times. A few weeks later, my daughter Marjorie's car broke down. I called Ken and he arranged for a tow to his dealership and gave Marjorie a ride back to UMass. When the car was repaired, he picked her up and brought her to retrieve her car. I went to Northampton a few weeks later to take Ken to lunch and thank him. The manager at the dealership told me that Ken stopped coming to work, that he just disappeared.

Ken surfaced again a year later, now living in an apartment in Greenfield. Coach Conway joined me in an attempt at an intervention. We climbed up the rickety three flights of stairs of a worn-down apartment building and knocked on the door. A woman answered and told us, "If you're such good friends, then Ken will know how to contact you." Then she slammed the door in our faces.

Ken passed away on September 10, 2012, at age forty-eight.

I was stunned when I heard the news. I know that those last few years were not the best for Ken. He definitely had his demons and his struggles, most of which I didn't know or understand. We had trained so many thousands of miles together. He was a really good kid and a close friend. It was so sad.

I like to remember Ken as "the Rookie," and the way it was back in the winter of 1982.

13

The Marathon

Being a runner in the late 1960s, people would often ask me, "Why are you running? Are you getting ready for the Boston Marathon?" In the springtime at local road races, the conversation was much the same: "Are you running Boston?" It seemed like most people equated distance running with marathons. They even referred to some road races as "mini-marathons." When my issue of *Distance Running News* (before it became *Runner's World*) arrived, it contained many articles about the marathon.

My first experience with a marathon was in 1968. Track season had ended and I ran the Holyoke Marathon. Holyoke was notorious for the uphill grind the last six miles. The race was held in the heat of the day and water stops were few and far between. It really was a pretty bad introduction to marathon running. Totally not ready for twenty-six miles, I staggered to the finish in a time of 3:26. I was fifteen years old.

It would be two years before I ran another marathon. I met Tom Derderian and Ed Walkwitz at local road races. Both were preparing for marathons and running a lot of training miles. Tom ran for UMass and went on to be an excellent marathoner, running a 2:19 marathon best and qualifying for the Olympic trials. He became the coach of the Greater Boston Track Club and also an accomplished writer for running magazines.

Tom later published an amazing book, *The History of the Boston Marathon*. Ed was a student at Springfield College and was into high-mileage training. In 1970, Ed took twenty minutes off his personal best to become the fourth American finisher at the Boston Marathon. Ed's time was 2:23. My training partner and long-time friend Frank McDonald ran a 2:54 in that same Boston race. Frank's time of 2:54 finished him 218th place and he was the third runner under eighteen to finish.

I kept thinking that I could run another marathon.

Someday, when the time was right.

I always liked the idea of being a marathon runner. It was unique and there weren't a lot of people doing it. I always felt there was a mystique about the distance: twenty-six miles and 385 yards. It was definitely challenging and required a real commitment and consistent training. My father took me to meet Rod Hochrein, a former Boston Marathon runner. Mr. Hochrein was an old-timer who worked at the student sport shop at Deerfield Academy.

I remember listening to his Boston Marathon tales and getting excited about running the distance. He told me about his favorite training course, the pumping station loop. My high school coach Pete Conway shared his stories with me of his marathon days running for the Boston Athletic Association and competing in the Yonkers Marathon.

My high school focus was on training and running road races in the summer and running cross-country in the fall. When cross-country season ended, it was back to running the roads with a little indoor track mixed in. The high school running season ended with spring track, and then the cycle began again. Road races were so much fun and you got a chance to meet lots of runners who all seemed to enjoy sharing training thoughts and ideas. Along with Tom Derderian and Ed Walkwitz, I met John Jarek, Russ Holt, Peter Stasz, and Roland Cormier, all veteran road racers. Frank and I would hang out after races and absorb information like sponges. Most of these guys were much older than us and after the race would offer us ice-cold beers, which we gladly accepted!

In 1970, I again ran the Holyoke Marathon. It was the day after the state track meet, where I finished sixth and failed to qualify for the New England Championship. Dealing with the emotional pain I was in, failing to achieve my long-time goal, I decided to add some physical pain to the mix. I entered the Holyoke Marathon the next day! Despite having not done any training runs over ten miles, I finished in 3:10, which was good for twenty-first place.

On the heels of Holyoke, I decided to train longer distances and add more mileage to my routine. Frank McDonald and I traveled to Boone, North Carolina, to compete in the Grandfather Mountain Marathon. On the insane mountainous course, I ran 3:26, finishing sixteenth. In the fall, I ran the New York City Marathon in brutal heat, finishing thirteenth in 2:56. A month later, I ran the Atlantic City Marathon. Atlantic City was the national championship and Ed, John Jarek, and I took the bronze medal as a team. I finished in twenty-first place, coming in at 2:50.

In the Greenfield area, there were many great runners training for marathons. Our evening winter training group recorded some impressive performances. Denny Tetreault ran a 2:25 in Boston and won several other marathons, including Holyoke and Clarence DeMar. Connie Putnam ran 2:48 at Boston and set a personal record at the Clarence DeMar, crossing the line in 2:46. Ed Porter ran ten straight Bostons. Lea Hayer ran in the Olympic trials in 1984. Mickey Campaniello ran ten Bostons and had a personal record of 2:46. It seemed like everyone around me was running marathons.

Over the next eight years I would run six more marathons before I came to the realization that I was not a marathon runner. Yes, it really took me that long.

In 1978, I trained a bit with Ed Strabel. Ed was a graduate student at Springfield College and a fitness instructor at West Point who was training for the Boston Marathon. During the winter of '78, I beat Ed in the mile and two-mile indoors. I beat him at the Amherst ten-mile race, too. In March, I finished ahead of Ed at the Holyoke Road Race. A few weeks later, at the Milk Run in Boston, I bested once Ed again.

During the winter, Jack Mahurin, my friend and exercise physiologist at Springfield College, put Ed and I through a VO2 Max test on the treadmill. VO2 Max is a performance test that's one of the key indicators of success for long-distance runners. Basically, it measures how many liters of oxygen you can utilize per kilogram of body weight. Ed and I both scored 68 max Vo2. Ed ran 2:17 at Boston that spring. My best would remain 2:47.

Even though I was very lean, I carried a lot of body weight—"Thunder Thighs Martino," as Rick Bayko described me in an issue of *Yankee Runner*. Bayko wrote, "It's amazing that a guy with weight-lifter's legs can run that fast." At my best, I carried a hundred fifty pounds on my 5'8" frame.

The other factor that worked against me in the marathon was my cooling system. To say that it's very efficient is an understatement. Profusely sweating in a three- to six-mile race was a great advantage to keep me cool. But during the marathon, this amount of water loss was definitely my enemy! Bill Rodgers once told a writer for *Runner's World* that I was "the world's greatest sweater."

I learned that in the marathon, you had to have patience, which is a trait I've never possessed. I found it hard to focus for the duration of the long race. What experience finally taught me is that I enjoyed and performed well at most distances up to a half-marathon. My 5K (14:35) and six-mile (29:54) times were very competitive, and I loved to compete. I loved to win road races, and when I couldn't win, I liked being right in the mix!

Eventually, I settled into my role as a road racer and left the marathon behind. The plain fact is that I was never as good as I wanted to be in the marathon. The further I raced after ten miles, the more my performance diminished. (See per-minute mile chart below.) I think the lesson to be learned is to find what distance suits you best and stick to it. It took a long time for me to learn that.

As Bill Rodgers says, "The marathon can humble you."

My Marathons
(from my training diary)

1967 Holyoke Marathon

Hot and no water. Idiot for running with no long-distance training.

Sophomore in high school. Last six miles were uphill!

Time: 3:26

1970 Holyoke Marathon

Hot!! Hardly any water. So sore and stiff, couldn't drive home.

Finished on the midway of the amusement park. We seemed to be one of the sideshows!

Ran this race after my failure to qualify for high school New England's the day before.

Rick Sherlund, Pete Wayman, and Jim Dejoy were my pit crew, driving around the course in *my* car drinking beer!

Time: 3:10

1970 Grandfather Mountain Marathon (Boone, North Carolina)

Crazy insane course!! Finished strong despite running uphill the last ten miles.

Frank McDonald and I spent all the money we made working at the Y camp for travel and food.

As the race ad stated, "beautiful, mountainous and devastating." Should have given us a clue!

Time: 3:26

1970 NYC Marathon

Not much water. Very hot day, eighty degrees. Central Park is brutally hilly!

Four big loops and one small loop.

Rick Sherlund and I had to walk downstairs backward, we were so sore afterwards. We were almost mugged in Central Park.

Time: 2:56 (thirteenth place)

1970 Atlantic City Marathon

Back and forth on the same straight road!

Finished on the boardwalk. Ed finished second.

Twenty-first place and bronze medal as a team.

Time: 2:50

1971 Boston Marathon

Hot! Felt terrible and was walking in Natick. Walked with Tom Derderian at ten miles.

Walked/jogged all the way to the finish. Amazing time, considering all the walking and the heat.

Time: 3:00

1971 Pavo Nurmi Marathon (Hurley, Wisconsin)

Hot and humid. Race started at 5:50 in the morning.

Hitchhiked to the race in northern Wisconsin.

Time: 3:15 (not bad for the heat/humidity!)

1977 Skylon International Marathon (Buffalo to Niagara)

Rick and Janet Sherlund traveled with me in my small pick-up truck.

We had fun on my CB Radio. Janet's "breaker, breaker, trucker boys!" got lots of attention from the truck drivers.

Finished next to Niagara Falls.

Time: 3:10 (best recollection; not in my diary)

1978 Ottawa Marathon (Canada)

Nice course. Felt comfortable, should have pushed harder. Too much energy left over at the end.

Stiffened up like a board afterwards. Needed help getting my warmups on.

Mickey Campaniello and Lou Soquet drove by us on a highway in Canada!

Time: 2:47 (personal record)

1978 NYC Marathon

Hot! Started out with Mike Connelly from Turners Falls.

Ended up in the medical tent at the finish, wicked dehydrated. Had to be lifted over the fencing because I couldn't walk.

As they were putting my IV in, I looked over at the cot next to me…and it was Mike!

Time: 3:05

Analysis of my pace per mile

1 mile	4:26
2 miles	4:50 per mile
3.1 miles	4:52 per mile
4.8 miles	4:55 per mile
5 miles	4:59 per mile
6 miles	4:59 per mile
6.2 miles	5:04 per mile
6.8 miles	4:59 per mile
10 miles	5:16 per mile
13.1 miles	5:23 per mile
20 miles	6:00 per mile
26.2 miles	6:23 per mile

14

Oasis in the Winter

Winter training in New England certainly has its challenges. Like all runners, I've run in snowstorms, sleet, brutal windchill temperatures, and cold rain. You really don't have a choice and, if you thought the way I did, winter was the time to get tougher and stronger than your competitors. I look back at my training logs and sometimes shake my head thinking, "How did I do that?" I didn't like running in bad weather, but I felt I had to do it.

Winter was the time my weekly mileage increased. I usually went from seventy miles per week to eighty, ninety, and upward of a hundred miles. Some of my winter log book entries looked like this:

6-mile run, flooded conditions, icy water up over my ankles.

10-mile run, very icy conditions, dark and cold out.

13-mile run, minus 30 wind chill, icy spots.

During conditions like that, you start to dream about running on a nice indoor track, free of the brutal conditions outside. During the winter of 1987, I started thinking about it seriously. I thought to myself, "If I could get indoors once a week, I could run some quality workouts to go along with my winter outdoor runs."

When I lived in Western Massachusetts, it was easy. I could go to UMass and run on the boards in Curry Hicks Cage almost any time I wanted. Now, living in the Boston area, I had to figure out where to go.

My first stop was Wellesley College. The new indoor facility was beautiful and I walked right in! It was snowing outside that day and I was able to run a decent workout of 400s, 800s and 400s inside. It was great not to worry about slipping on ice. The next week, it was snowing again and I went back to Wellesley for more. This time: 800-yard repeats.

As I drove home in the snow, I thought that this weekly reprieve from winter was just what I needed. The following week, it was brutally cold and, again, I headed off to Wellesley. I walked past the control desk, looking confident, and began my warm-up. A few minutes later, a security guard came onto the track and stopped me. He said something like, "You don't belong here," and proceeded to escort me off the track.

So much for my winter reprieve.

I called my friend, Fred Doyle. Fred was a fantastic runner, first for the University of New Hampshire and then for the Greater Boston Track Club. Fred's résumé included a 2:19 marathon and a 4:05 mile. Fred was working for Nike and was also interested in doing some quality indoor workouts. He said we could always get into Boston University. The track was elevated off the ground, with eight laps to the mile and high banked turns. It was inside a field house, which was not very well lit—but there was no snow, ice, or wind, so I was in! Fred and I charged into a workout that included 400s in sixty-eight-plus, 800s in 2:23, and 600s in 1:47.

The following week, we went over to MIT and found it easy to get in. There was only one other person running on the track, whom we recognized right away: Mickey Roche, the Boston Police Commissioner. We had another great session. Fred planned the workouts, which were always different and challenging. I never knew what to expect, but I knew I was getting fitter and fitter each week. I couldn't wait for spring and the chance to test myself in some local road races.

The next two weeks, we alternated between BU and MIT, continuing to improve our fitness. The MIT track was tough on the turns and BU was always dark. Fred mentioned that there was still another alternative: Harvard University.

At the time, Harvard had the finest indoor track in New England, with a very fast surface and gentle banked turns. The back stretch wall was all glass so you could look out at the elements that you were escaping from.

The question was, could we get in?

I arrived at the Harvard track and nervously walked into the entranceway. There was no Fred but there was an older security man working the desk. I walked up and said, "I'm meeting my friend Fred Doyle here." I introduced myself and he told me his name was Jack. He proceeded to tell me my buddy was already inside. When I found Fred he was already doing some stretching. I asked him how he got in. He said he'd simply asked Jack if Bill Rodgers had arrived yet.

Bill wasn't as adventurous as we were. Taking no chances, Bill had come armed with a letter from Albert Gordon, the Wall Street businessman who had donated the track to Harvard. The letter stated, "Please allow Bill Rodgers to use the track facility."

Bill had been at a dinner at the New York Athletic Club where he was seated with Mr. Gordon. During their farewell, Mr. Gordon told Bill to let him know if there was anything he could do for him.

Bill had Albert Gordon; Fred and I had Jack. We were in!

We felt like we owned the place. One day I came in and Jack said, "Your buddy's in the locker room." I started walking down the hall and Jack said, "No, not down there…he's in *that* one," pointing to the door with "Private/Officials" written on it. "How great is this?" I thought. "Now we have our own private locker room!"

That day, the track was more crowded than usual. All of a sudden, onto the track came Jack with security guards. Apparently, most of the runners on the track snuck in through an open door. Can you imagine the nerve of some people?! They threw out almost everyone except a few Harvard students…and Fred and me. Jack told security, "Those two are alright." When we were leaving, Joe Catalano, a local coach, was arriving with some of his athletes. He had a box of donuts for Jack, which he thought would be his ticket in. Jack said, "Thanks for the donuts…but you can't come in!"

The sessions at Harvard kept getting better and better and I could tell I was going to have a solid spring on the road racing scene. On our final workout of the season, Fred planned a tough workout of 400s, 800s, and three-quarter-mile repeats, ending with a series of 200s at a fairly brisk pace of thirty-three to thirty-four seconds. As we did our workout, we saw Scott Wedman and Bill Walton in the center of the track on the tennis court, playing a match against Walton's wife.

Scott Wedman was in the later stages of his career when the Boston Celtics acquired him. He stepped in big-time for the

Celtics. Walton is, of course, a legend, but that day, Bill and Scott received a royal stomping from Susie Walton!

At the end of their match, Scott recognized Fred from some Nike appearances they'd done together, so we took a break and chatted a bit. Scott asked what we were doing and we told him we were finishing with some 200s. He asked, "Mind if I join you?" For a big guy (6'7") he ran very well. I remember going around the banked turn and looking up at him, thinking he looked eight feet tall!

During the summer, Fred and I received postcards from Ireland, signed "Your friend, Jack Cochran." It took us a bit to figure out who it was because we'd never known security guard Jack's last name. The following winter, when we showed up for our new season, Jack greeted us with a bottle of Irish whiskey! Fred made sure Jack's grandkids had Nike T-shirts and Jack was comfortable in his new Nike shoes.

At the start of our third year, we arrived at the track to find a new guy there. Fred immediately asked him where Jack was. "Jack retired," he barked back at us. Fred asked his name and he told us it was Tom. We told him we were friends of Jack's. After a few minutes, he grumpily told us to go on in. That night I called Bill and asked him if he still had that letter from Mr. Gordon, just to be safe!

15

To Finish Is to Win

In 1976, a new type of athletic competition was held in the Berkshires: a triathlon named the Great Josh Billings RunAground. This was one of the first triathlons in the country. The event combined bicycle racing with canoeing and running.

Josh Billings was the pen name for American humorist Henry Wheeler Shaw. Shaw was born in the Berkshires in 1818 and was well-known for his witty quotes. Some of his more famous quotes are, "The rarest thing a man ever duz iz the best he can," and "There are two things in life for which we're never truly prepared: twins." It was his quote, "To finish is to win," that became the mantra for the Josh Billings event.

I'm not sure exactly how we found out about the event, but my brother Greg pulled our team together. I would do the running, Greg would bike, and Jim Allen and Mickey Campaniello would team up to paddle the canoe. Greg wasn't a bike racer and Mickey and Jim had never been in a canoe together. So Greg, a great athlete himself, began a daily training regimen of riding his ten-speed bike while Jim and Mickey began paddling an aluminum canoe together every few days in Barton Cove.

Jim was the physical director at the Greenfield Y and Mickey was his assistant. Both were excellent swimmers and very well-known as swim instructors. In fact, Jim taught me how to swim when I was seven years old. He actually taught most of the kids in the county how to swim.

One early evening as they were finishing a canoeing workout, they accidentally tipped the canoe over. They were laughing and joking and trying to upright the canoe, having a great time in the water until a neighbor looked out the window, thinking they were drowning! The woman called rescue and before long, they had a fire truck, ambulance, police, and a rescue boat there to assist them. They assured the rescuers that they were fine and got the canoe uprighted and paddled to shore. Everything ended well… until the newspaper came out the next day with a highlighted story about the rescue from the Connecticut River! The two most well-known aquatic instructors in the county were in the news… and not in an ideal way.

We made our reservations to stay in a Lenox motel the night before the Josh Billings race. When we arrived, we picked up the registration packet and got involved with some carbohydrate-loading at the welcome reception. Dinner followed and the brews flowed. Arriving back at our motel, Greg was concerned that someone might steal the canoe, so we decided to lift it up to the second-floor balcony and put it in their room. In the middle of the night, Jim got up to go to the bathroom, tripped over the canoe, and landed on the floor. His first thought, still fuzzy from the pre-race party was, "I think there's a canoe in our room."

The first Josh began with the runners leaving Mount Greylock Regional High School, where they passed off to the cyclists at the

Brodie Mountain Ski Resort. The cyclists rode twenty-seven miles through Pittsfield, finishing at "the Bowl," aka Lake Mahkeenac, a 372-acre artificial lake just south of Tanglewood. The cyclists then handed off to the canoeists, who paddled five miles around the Bowl. (In future events, the Josh would begin with cycling, followed by canoeing, with the last leg being the run.) At the completion of the event, there was a post-race party held on the grounds of a restaurant across from the Tanglewood music pavilion. In the coming years, this party would be appropriately known as a "bash."

Our race began and the pack of runners started off. Right after the gun went off, a blond-haired and very tan runner gave me a hard high elbow to my shoulder. In all my years of running, this had never happened before. I yelled out to him, "Hey watch it!" His response? "If you don't like it, start at the back of the pack." I chased after him…but was never able to catch him. He crossed the line first and I came in second. After the run, I went up to him to have a discussion about his behavior and remember Mickey and Jim holding me back.

As I found out later, his name was Mark Sisson, and all was forgiven and forgotten between us after a few brews at the post-race party. Sisson's cyclist was Billy Farrell, from Greenfield, a great competitive biker and an amazing ski racer. I remember Billy racing cars with his ten-speed bike down Federal Street in Greenfield on Friday nights. In the Josh he flew to the finish and, combined with their canoe team of first-class paddlers, won easily. Greg held his own and Mickey and Jim paddled us to a top-five finish. We were very pleased, wearing our Greenfield T-shirts, printed by Don Clark from Clark's Sport Shop, my employer at the time and our team sponsor.

Then it was off to the post-race party at a place called Alice's Restaurant, just like the Arlo Guthrie song. The beer was flowing from self-serve taps and you could smell the burgers on the grill. I went over to the woman cooking to thank her, only to discover that she was *the* Alice, the one from the song, cooking my burger!

I thought this was the coolest thing ever and went to my teammates with the news. Greg and Mickey thought it was amazing, too, but Jim had no idea who Alice was, as he didn't know about the story of Alice's Restaurant. I sang a little of the song for Jim, hoping it would jog his memory. "You know, 'You can get anything you want at Alice's Restaurant'?" I told him about the Thanksgiving dinner, Alice Brock and Arlo Guthrie, Officer Obie, and the 8x10 glossy photos of the garbage. Jim still had no clue. Jim, always wanting to learn new things, headed over to the grill. He spent the next thirty minutes talking to Alice and learning all about *Alice's Restaurant Massacree*.

We were hooked, and the Josh Billings race became an annual event for us for many years.

The second year, we decided we needed a team name. We were at the Franklin County Fair and it was approaching closing time. A big crowd had gathered around the dunk tank, where an obnoxious guy was sitting on the seat of the tank, brutally insulting people so that they threw the baseball so hard they couldn't hit the target. He kept saying, "I'm high and dry." We bought Jim some tickets and the guy began calling Jim an "old man with a rubber arm." No one could knock this guy into the water! I saw Mickey talking to the guy in charge and noticed him giving the guy some money. All of a sudden, Mickey hurdled the table and sprinted up to hit the button, knocking the guy into the water. The crowd went wild and our team name became High and Dry!

The Josh grew to amazing proportions and the bash became its signature event. It had beer trucks, food stations, and a stage with a band. Tanglewood became the permanent finish line. The

Greenfield contingent was right in the middle of the mix! We were always the first to arrive, securing a prime location for watching the finish and being in the thick of the action.

Not only were we the first to arrive, but we were always the last to leave, too. We competed hard and really enjoyed the post-race bash. At one event, my friend Ed Porter came up to me with a big grin on his face. He told me to follow him around to the back of the beer pavilion, where he showed me a cigar box full of beer tickets, which he'd somehow "mysteriously" found. We spent the rest of the afternoon being very popular, as we bought rounds of beer for ourselves and all our new friends!

There was perhaps a little too much alcohol involved in our post-Josh receptions. Fortunately, we all had designated drivers. One year, Ken Rillings, my brother Greg, and Jim Allen somehow got invited to a post-race party at a state senator's home in Stockbridge. Ken was a big, muscular, burly guy who we nicknamed "the Bear." Upon entering the home, they noticed that everyone else was dressed up. The High and Dry crew attracted attention from the get-go. Ken walked up to the hors d'oeuvres table, picked up a knife, and stabbed a large round of cheese, lifting it up in the air complete with pirate sound effects, "Aarrr!" Meanwhile, Jim went missing for a while. When he reappeared, he had a cut on his head and scratches on his arms. Apparently, Jim had opened a door to use the bathroom. There was an addition being added on to the main house, and when Jim stepped into "the bathroom," he had rolled down an embankment.

As the years went by, the canoes became more sophisticated. Aluminum tubs became obsolete and ultra-lightweight Kevlar became the competitive norm. The Josh grew bigger and better, much more competitive.

In 1983, we entered the race in the family division. My younger brother Tony would cycle and Greg would canoe with our father. I anchored with the six-mile run. Our main competition was the Rillings family from Shelburne. Ken Rillings, Jr. was a competitive cyclist and his father Ken Sr., along with his mother Nancy, would canoe. Ken Sr. was my brother's regular competition canoe partner. Their daughter, Kara, was an excellent high school runner who would anchor the team.

Ken Jr. finished in the first pack of bikes, opening up a big lead on the bike leg. Tony, who was just a teenager, rode as hard as he could. Greg and my father closed the gap a bit in the water, but the Rillings team had over a ten-minute lead on us. I ran as hard as I could in the heat and as I turned into the Tanglewood driveway, I saw Kara staggering toward the finish line. The ninety-degree heat had taken its toll, and I passed her with less than a hundred yards to go. The Martinos were the 1983 family division winners! I remember how proud it felt to go up onto the stage with my father and brothers to receive our award.

The Josh Billings race definitely brings back fond remembrances. From that first event forty-five years ago, with Alice at the grill cooking the hamburgers, to the competition, fun, and fellowship of all the races that followed, the Josh will always be a classic.

Josh Billings said it best: "To finish is to win."

16

Camping

Summer is the perfect time for camping. In the summer of 1993, Bill Rodgers took us camping at New Hampshire's Mount Washington Hotel and Resort as the first Bill Rodgers Running and Fitness Camp was launched. One of Bill's relatives worked at the resort and suggested that the hotel was the ideal location for a running camp. After a few meetings with the marketing people, the camp was a go!

Bill's camp would give participants the opportunity to learn about things like training best practices, nutrition, strength training, injury prevention, and running shoes, and they would receive individual coaching. Perhaps most important of all, participants would have the chance to run with the "King of the Roads" himself.

The Mount Washington Hotel was an amazingly beautiful location. The historic setting in the White Mountains was incredibly picturesque. At the time, the hotel was falling into disrepair and in need of a serious upgrade. Also, the place was not winterized, which limited the amount of business it could do. Still, it had a quaint charm about it, and the staff was very hospitable. I remember one elderly elevator operator who was quite entertaining. I can still hear him saying, "Going down to the fun floor!" which was the lower level with an ice cream shop, arcade, retail stores, and a nice restaurant for lunch. On the back porch of the hotel, you could sit and watch the cog rail train make its way to the peak of Mount Washington and follow its progress by the smoke billowing from its stacks.

The hotel also had two golf courses, which were perfect to run around. A beautiful trail ran along the side of a boulder-strewn roaring stream, which was crystal clear. There was a bridge about four miles up the trail where we could cross the river and connect to the cog railway road. Across the road from the hotel was the Breton Mountain ski area, which had a challenging trail that led to a freshly-mowed ski slope. I still remember Tom Fleming skipping down the mountain singing, "The hills are alive with the sound of music." Everywhere you turned, it was beautiful. Soon we were all skipping down the mountain and singing along with Tom.

The staff members Bill recruited were amazing. Joan Benoit Samuelson, winner of the gold medal in the 1984 Olympics, former world record holder, and running icon, ran with the campers and held several clinics during the three-day camp. Nancy Clark, the well-known sports nutritionist and author, planned the dinner menu and gave a nutrition presentation. Tom Fleming provided world-class coaching. Greg Meyer, who at the time was the last American to win the Boston Marathon, conducted clinics on cross-country and trail running. Bill's brother Charlie managed the Bill Rodgers Running Center at the Faneuil Hall in Boston. Charlie brought his vast knowledge of footwear to the camp, along with lots of samples for people to try. My responsibility was to run a strength-training clinic, helping runners avoid injuries and improve their performance. We had the perfect staff and location for a successful camp.

Unfortunately, we had small attendance at our first two camps. The ratio of staff to campers was one to three. Perhaps the marketing didn't reach the right places, or maybe the Mount Washington Hotel was too far away for participants. In any case, it was a first-class experience for those who did attend—and a great vacation for the staff! Every morning we went on a group run, followed by the most amazing breakfast buffet you could imagine. Bill and I both agreed that it was the best bacon we've ever eaten. We attracted a bit of attention with our loaded plates! We had several clinics in the morning and then met up for the afternoon run. We ran on the golf courses and wooded trails. It was truly beautiful running.

We had only one mishap. A high school girl, who was dropped off each day by her father, took a wrong turn and didn't return from the evening run. We took golf carts out searching for her, and after about two hours, just as it was getting dark, we found her. It was pretty intense for a while there, though it all worked out all right in the end.

The dinners at the hotel were experiences unto themselves! You had to dress up for dinner, including wearing a jacket. Camp staff and campers sat together and there was a separate kids' table. Our daughter Marjorie sat with Greg's, Joan's, and Tom's kids. When I look at the pictures of the kids at the table, I'm amazed. They're all grown up now and some have kids of their own. I remember how well-behaved they were and how much fun they had when the Mount Washington Orchestra played a medley of children's songs through dinner. While having dessert each night, a singer by the name of Tad performed with the orchestra. Tad was a large man with an incredible powerful voice. He got many people out on the dance floor. After dancing a bit, we had another important activity to participate in: moose hunting!

After dinner, we would all rush to our rooms, changed clothes, then meet in the lobby, ready to moose hunt. Moose hunting involved driving our cars slowly down the road in the breakdown lane, turning on our high beams, and looking for moose. We all kept track of how many we saw, and it soon became a competition.

One evening, Ginger and I drove up a desolate back road where we'd seen moose on a bike ride earlier that day. On our bike ride, we'd stopped at a marshland and there, fifty feet away, was a mother moose with her newborns. It was obvious she wasn't happy to see us, so we quickly went on our way. That evening, as we drove up that same stretch of road, there were no lights, and it seemed like we were in the middle of nowhere. All of a sudden, we heard the loud rumbling of a truck engine and spotlights came shining at us. We had no clue what was going on and were a little frightened. It turned out to be Tom and Greg! They'd taken moose hunting to a new level, purchasing plug-in spotlights for Greg's SUV. But they made so much noise that any moose in the area would be long gone.

Camp also included a lot of time for leisure activities and one day, Bill and I decided to go trout fishing at the beautiful, clear stream on the property. I convinced Ginger to hike down to the stream and watch a couple of "expert fishermen" in action. Sure enough, Bill had a tug on his line and a second later, I got one. We were both excited as we reeled in our catch. However, we soon realized just what it was we had both caught…we'd hooked each other!

I remember Ginger rolling her eyes and walking away, shaking her head. Can't really say I blame her.

The running camp was a perfect vacation. Our daughter Hileary was also able to join us, as well as my father and my stepmother Barbara, who loved sitting out on the massive porch in the comfortable rocking chairs. Even our new pet hamster enjoyed the Mount Washington, getting to see the lobby from Ginger's shirt pocket.

We conducted one more camp that summer, at the exclusive Equinox Hotel, in Manchester, Vermont. This camp was better attended, with about thirty campers. Manchester was an awesome place to run. We could run along the Battenkill River, which is famous for trout fishing. Our running loop went by the summer home of Mary Todd Lincoln.

The highlight of that camp was a visit from Dr. George Sheehan. A cardiologist, Dr. Sheehan, was also the guru of the running movement in the 1970s and 1980s. He was a bestselling author and his writings were an inspiration to all runners. Dr. Sheehan was at this point in the late stages of his cancer battle and was showing signs that he was in pain. I had the opportunity to meet him and thank him for all he did for our sport of running. At the welcoming dinner, he spoke for about thirty minutes and the room was totally quiet. He captivated us with a summary of what he'd learned on his journey. The next evening, he sat on a panel discussion with the lineup of Rodgers, Fleming, and our other coaches, Samuelson and Meyer. To me, it was the history of running all packed into one room. The following morning, Dr. Sheehan's son, George the Third, drove him back to New Jersey. It was the last public appearance of his life. Dr. Sheehan passed away on November 1, 1993.

The following year we conducted two more running camps at the Ascutney Mountain Resort in Vermont. My wife Ginger joined our staff and we enjoyed another great family summer experience. The camp was a success, but it didn't compare to the atmosphere of the Mount Washington. The Mount Washington had character throughout, from the elderly elevator operator who was dressed in his suit and bow tie every day, to the orchestra who played for us every night.

On our last day at Mount Washington Bill met the new owner, who told him big things would soon be happening at the hotel. It was going to be updated and winterized, with a plan to become a year-round destination resort. He invited Bill and me to pose for a picture with him.

That fall, my Aunt Denise took a tour of the hotel with her husband Donny. The tour guide brought them to the entranceway of the dining room, where they saw pictures on the "wall of fame," highlighting all the famous people who stayed there. My aunt was looking at the wall when all of a sudden she loudly said, "Donny, that's Joey!"

Sure enough, there was the picture of the new owner, Bill, and me, on the Mount Washington wall of fame!

17

Millrose Games

I'd always wanted to attend the Millrose Games in New York City at Madison Square Garden. I enjoyed indoor track and had conversations about it with several friends, who were interested in the Millrose Games as well. The Games have run since 1914 on a steeply banked, eleven-laps-to-the-mile track in the Garden. The feature event of the evening is the Wanamaker Mile race, which has attracted the greatest milers in the world.

In February 2004 I connected our group—friends of mine, but most of them strangers to each other. The "Millrose Five" (eventually the "Millrose Six") consisted of Jon Barnes, Bill Rodgers, Tom Fleming, Rick Sherlund, and myself. I sent out a weekly newsletter to build up enthusiasm and assign responsibilities to everyone in the group.

Jon was my former board chair at the Y and a well-respected banker in Rhode Island who ran for Lafayette College and had already competed in the Millrose Games. He had run a 2:28:06 marathon at Boston in the days when a great time like that didn't make the top two hundred! Jon was assigned to lunch duty and he volunteered to bring his collection of classic running magazines. Tom's job was to come up with the tickets, as he had a long relationship with the New York Athletic Club (NYAC). Rick took charge of the hotel rooms and agreed to host us for a pre-event dinner at Nick & Stef's, a fine steakhouse with a private entryway into the garden. Bill would bring the Boston newspapers and, importantly, promised to be on time! I agreed to drive, with Jon acting as my navigator.

The good news was that Bill *was* on time. The bad news? It was snowing like crazy and the roads were a mess. After Bill and I picked up Jon in Rhode Island, we decided to park and take the train from Providence to New York. It was a beautiful train ride along the Connecticut shore and we watched the snow coming down hard. On board the train we met John Thomas, the former Olympic high jumper who would be officiating the Millrose Games.

We arrived in New York, checked into our hotel, and then rendezvoused with Rick and Tom at our restaurant. Rick carefully reviewed the wine list and chose two fine wines. Our meals were terrific and when the waiter brought the check, Jon grabbed it. Rick said, "Jon, I've got that." Jon replied that it was his treat, he wanted to thank Rick for the hotel rooms and hospitality. Jon stared at the check, signed it, and then we were off to the Games. Jon had that deer-in-the-headlights look in his eyes. I remember him saying that he just spent $1,200 on dinner and most of it was the two bottles of wine! The funny thing is that Jon doesn't drink wine. One of the wines—a 1997 Harlan Estate—had given Jon a new nickname, "Harlan Barnes."

We all really enjoyed the meet and each other's company. Between Bill and Tom, it seemed like they knew everyone in the Garden. The legendary miler, Jim Ryun, and his wife Ann sat right in front of us. Tom really enjoyed reacquainting with old friends. He introduced me to Larry Rawson, the ESPN Emmy award–winning sports commentator. We attended the NYAC after-event party and enjoyed conversation with lots of interesting people in the track and field world.

We had such a great time, we decided to make it an annual event. As we talked about the following year in the lobby of the Hotel Pennsylvania, we noticed a large number of two-wheelers being pushed into the lobby loaded with crates of dogs! Apparently the hotel was about to host the Westminster Dog Show. One woman there was with a beautiful Newfoundland, which was very playful with me. It kept coming over for attention. The following Monday evening I received a call from Bill saying, "Quick! Turn on the dog show—your dog just won the championship!"

The following year, Bill promised he would take care of the train tickets, as well as the meet tickets. We were all a little skeptical, but Bill seemed pretty confident. Bill had met a train conductor at the Disney Marathon and the guy gave him his card and stated if Bill ever needed anything, to give him a call.

We felt a little uneasy getting onto a train with no tickets. We stowed our bags away and watched a conductor coming up the aisle, collecting tickets. Being ticketless, we were sweating it a bit. All of a sudden, Bill's contact, the head conductor, arrived. He said to Bill, "I've been looking all over for you! I have some seats in first class for you guys." We were off to first class! During our train ride, we also made our way through the engine room to the cockpit. The engineer was a runner and wanted to meet Bill. I must admit, it was a pretty interesting experience in the small cockpit as we traveled at ninety miles per hour.

The next year, we again traveled by train—but this time with a folded-up ticket stub with "Please carry my friends from Providence to NYC" hand-written on the back by the head conductor. We also had a new member of our team, Fred Doyle.

Fred ran in the Millrose Games in 1980 as a member of the Greater Boston Track Club 4x880 relay team and won a Millrose medal for finishing third. We decided that Fred's initiation would include providing us with appropriate Millrose Six gear, seeing as he worked for Nike and could get a good deal. Fred came through big-time and we were off in style with our Millrose Six sweatshirts.

The paper ticket worked and we were enjoying our train ride, when all of a sudden we heard a young lady's voice call out, "Boston Billy! Boston Billy!" I looked out into the aisle and there was a woman about twenty-five years old, staggering through the train with a glass of wine, looking for Boston Billy. Apparently she'd been in the club car with a group of guys who told her a famous athlete was on the train. In her inebriated state, she set off with her glass of wine as her compass to find Boston Billy!

The woman stopped at the seat across from us and asked the people there if they knew Boston Billy. The gentleman she'd addressed pointed our way. Oh, boy. Staggering over to us, she asked who Boston Billy was and Jon, pouring fuel on the fire, showed her a magazine with Bill on the cover. She was shocked. I remember her plopping down in the seat next to me and saying to Bill, "Boston Billy, tell me all about it." Needless to say, we couldn't wait to get into Penn Station and away from this bizarre scene. For the rest of the day we hounded Bill with calls of "Boston Billy." It drove him nuts.

The 2009 Games were our last of a six-year annual outing. We chose to travel by car and with Jon skillfully driving, we made our way into Manhattan. We were at a stop light when a car pulled up next to us and honked the horn. It was Tom, on his way to the hotel to meet us. I kept thinking, "How is it possible to run into your friend at a traffic light in the middle of New York City?!"

We gathered at the hotel for pre-dinner cocktails. Tom asked Bill if he had the meet tickets and Bill said we'd pick them up at another hotel from "some guy." A decision was made for Bill and me to skip cocktails and seek out our tickets. We went to the other hotel, but no one seemed to know who "this guy" was. Finally, Bill remembered the guy's last name, who, as it turned out, was not answering his phone. One of the hotel employees led us to his room, where we knocked and knocked but got no answer. It wasn't looking good. In desperation, I suggested we go to the will-call window at the garden. As we walked up to the window, the attendant said, "Mr. Rodgers, I have some tickets for you!"

The dinner at Nick & Stef's was, as usual, fantastic. We had the same waiter as in years past and great food and wine. Harlan Barnes kept his hands in his pockets when the check arrived.

The Games were wonderful, but what I enjoyed most was watching and meeting the folks who came over to our section to say hello to Bill and Tom. I think we all got a kick out of that. As usual, Fred kept us decked out in new team uniforms. In 2009, it was Saucony jackets, as Fred had retired from Nike and started a new role with Saucony. Dennis Mitchell, the Olympic gold medal sprinter, sat next to me for a while. Dennis told me that, growing up as a young black athlete, he admired Tom because of his work ethic. Dennis was dressed to the nines! He wore a black silky shirt, black pants, red tie, white shoes, and a black velour jacket. During one of the lulls between events, Dennis got up to leave. I'll never forget Tom shouting to him, "Dennis, the next time you take things from my closet, ask me first!"

I've always felt good about connecting the Millrose Six together. It became more than a track meet; it was an annual reunion of friends who liked track and field and really enjoyed being together.

18

Tom Fleming

When I think about the Boston Marathon, I think about my dear friend Tom Fleming. Tom loved the Boston Marathon more than anyone. He said many times it was the one race he always wanted to win; he'd take a Boston win over an Olympic medal. Tom finished second twice and third once, among other top-ten finishes. He always made the race interesting, going to the front and pushing the pace. As Bill Rodgers put it, "Tom loved being in the mix."

My Tom Fleming story begins in October of 1970. Back in Western Massachusetts, I was training with a Springfield College student from South Hadley by the name of Ed Walkwitz. Ed had been on a tear since finishing twelfth in the Boston Marathon the previous April. Based on that performance, Ed was selected to attend the Olympic Training Camp at Washington State University in Pullman, Washington. The idea was to bring together the top U.S. runners to train for a month.

Ed started sending me postcards telling me things like, "Ran thirty-one miles today, 140 for the week." Ed was having an incredible experience and gaining great confidence. When he returned from camp, he drove up to Greenfield to do ten-mile runs along the Green River with my buddy Frank McDonald and me.

In October, the National Marathon Championship was being held in Atlantic City, New Jersey. Ed was one of the favorites to win. Together with John Jarek, a mutual friend from Chicopee, we loaded into Ed's brand new yellow VW bug and headed to New Jersey. We had no plan, no money, and no reservations, but we had plenty of time and enthusiasm. We left on a Friday for a Sunday race. When we hit New Jersey, Ed mentioned that his roommate Tom from the Olympic Training Camp lived in Bloomfield. Tom said that if Ed was ever in the area, he was welcome to stay with him and his family. We stopped at a pay phone and called Tom Fleming.

Tom's mom welcomed us and invited us to stay the night. They made plans for Tom's sister Joanne to stay at a friend's house so John and I could stay in her room. Tom's father, Joe, suggested that we all drive into the city in the morning and watch Tom run a cross-country race against the Coast Guard Academy. Tom finished second (which was the only time he lost a race at Van Cortland Park). What I remember most is Tom and his father analyzing and talking about the race all the way back to Jersey. It was quite a lively conversation.

Atlantic City was great, despite arriving literally two minutes before the starting gun. They actually held the race up as we pinned on our numbers! Ed finished second; John, fifteenth; and I was twenty-second. I think we also placed second as a team. When we were in our youth, recovery was so quick. The following weekend, I amazingly ran third in the junior college division of the Albany Invitational cross-country meet. I was starting out on a warm-down jog after the race when I heard someone calling my name. Tom Fleming was warming down with his Patterson State teammates. He invited me to run along with them.

Over the years, I often traveled to Bloomfield to train with Tom. I'd show up for the evening run, which was ten miles. Tom ran hard and would really tax my ability. Tom used to call it the "seventy-minute workout," which included a ten-mile run, a shower, fresh clothes, and opening a Coors Light, all in seventy minutes! I slept in the spare room where Tom kept all his running memorabilia. Tom had the greatest library of running books you could ever imagine, with many of his books signed by the author. I would stay up half the night reading them. The next morning, we'd be out the door for another ten miles. It was always amazing how easy my training runs felt when I returned home.

Tom was so Jersey street-wise. One morning, we headed out the door for a run. As we stepped outside, a guy dressed in a black suit approached us. He told us he was an insurance investigator and that there was an accident in front of the apartment the day before. He asked Tom about it. Tom said he didn't see anything and off we went on our run. A few steps into the run, Tom said, "I saw the whole thing but I'm not getting involved in that."

In the early eighties, Tom often came up to my hometown of Greenfield. We ran on a hard-packed dirt road along the beautiful Green River. Tom ran running clinics for me at the Greenfield Y, where I was the Fitness Director. We even cooked up the Tom Fleming Two-Hundred-Mile Challenge. Tom owned a specialty running store in Bloomfield called Tom Fleming's Running Room. The distance from the Y in Greenfield to Tom's store was two hundred miles. I thought the challenge was a great way to keep our Y joggers going in the winter. I teamed up with Fred Doyle, my friend from Nike, who printed up the most beautiful

Tom Fleming Two-Hundred-Mile Challenge T-shirts. Tom came to Greenfield and handed out over a hundred T-shirts to the successful joggers at a nice reception. Tom said something personal to each person as he handed them their shirt.

I introduced Tom to Milt Borofsky. Milt owned the local Howard Johnson's hotel and restaurant. Milt also happened to have six of the best seats in the old Boston Garden. Milt was always offering me his tickets, usually saving one for himself, just in case. Tom loved the Celtics so they hit it off. When I moved to Newton in 1984, Tom often flew up on People's Express, met us at the game, and then flew back to Jersey. He was a Jersey boy with a shiny green Celtics jacket!

My fondest Celtics memory was after a game, when Tom told us to go ahead to the restaurant and he'd meet us there. Thirty minutes later, he walked in with the entire NBA officiating crew: Bob Delaney, Jess Kersey, and the rookie referee. Tom knew Bob through Eddie Silverman, a high school running friend of Tom's, and a terrific high school miler. After Bob Delaney's father retired as a captain of the New Jersey State Police, Eddie brought him into the family business, SOS Security, where Eddie was CEO.

Bob also joined the New Jersey State Police and after a year and a half, he was selected to go undercover and infiltrate the mob on the New Jersey waterfront. He became Bobby Covert and he left his former life for almost three years. It's an amazing story so well told in his 2008 book, *Covert: My Years Infiltrating the Mob*. After he retired from the state police, Bob became an NBA referee for over twenty years.

Tom stayed at my apartment in Natick one weekend in March of 1985. He said he was going on a long run on Sunday with Bill Rodgers and asked if I'd like to join them. Although I wasn't fit for a long run, I said yes immediately. It's funny how things work out in life: Tom, great friends with Bill, and Tom and I, the same. The three of us began a friendship that lasted thirty-two years together—The Three Amigos.

To say Tom's passing rocked us big-time is an understatement. He was bigger than life. I always thought we would grow old together. At his memorial service, the outpouring of love and loss was incredible. Tom touched so many so deeply.

Tom was devoted to his kids and to his mother. He called his mother every single day, without exception, no matter where he was.

Every Marathon Monday, many who love the sport will think of Tom and smile, remembering his quote: "Somewhere, someone in the world is training when you are not. When you race him, he will win."

19

Toast to the Ones We Lost

One of the best things about running is the relationships you develop along the way. Something about a run with your friends opens up the freedom and opportunity to really get to know each other. Sharing thoughts and stories seems to make the miles go by more easily.

This is my attempt to toast the ones we lost along the way.

When you lose someone you shared so much time with on the road, someone you remember as being active and full of life, it's pretty tough to deal with. A void is opened that never fully closes. It hits you hard when one of your running mates falls.

During the winter of 1978, I was training at 6:00 p.m. after my work at Clark's Sport Shop. Like clockwork, I would arrive home and change into my Gore-Tex winter running clothes and jog-a-lite reflective vest, grab my lightweight disposable flashlight, and head out for my ten- to twelve-mile run. My usual route was down to the Greenfield swimming pool and through the meadows to the pumping station, mostly pitch-black with very few street lights. It would have been impossible to navigate without my flashlight. After running through the wooden covered bridge, I'd make my way back towards town on Leyden Road. To this day, I don't know how I did this night after night. It was so dark, cold, and desolate. So many things could have gone wrong.

One January night I ran alone, listening to the crunching sound my shoes made in the newly-fallen snow. I was watching the pattern of my light, which made its way from the ground to the horizon. All of a sudden, I looked ahead and saw a light coming toward me. I heard a crunch-crunch-crunch in the snow as the light became brighter. It was another human being!

We both stopped about ten feet from each other, unsure of the situation. We were so bundled up, neither of us was easily recognizable. After getting through the initial shock of running into another runner in the pitch-black in the middle of nowhere, we introduced ourselves. His name was Denny Tetreault.

I knew of Denny, as he was a member of the Greenfield High School 1964 state cross-country championship team. Denny told me he was training for the Boston Marathon. He turned around and ran back to town with me. It felt so much more comfortable running in the wilderness with a partner.

Over the next five years, Denny and I ran thousands of miles together. We continued to run in the dark after work, making the pumping station loop a regular route. Together, we competed in many road races, track workouts, and long Sunday runs. I helped Denny's speed and he helped me log the heavy miles, sometimes over a hundred miles per week. We were perfect for each other. In distances under ten miles, I would dominate. Distances over ten miles were definitely Denny's strength. Denny would get stronger and stronger the longer the distance. He ran over thirty marathons, including winning the Clarence DeMar and the Holyoke Marathons. He set a personal best of 2:25 at

Boston. Denny finished in the top three in the national fifty-kilometer championship.

When I left Greenfield for the Boston area in 1985, Denny was running strong. Sometime after that, we lost track of each other. I tried to reach out several times but couldn't find him. He had left the Greenfield area and it seemed like he just disappeared.

In 2012, I received an email from a friend who had learned of Denny's passing. I felt so sad that I wasn't able to reconnect with him. Reading the obituary, I saw that Denny remarried and had been living on the North Shore of Boston. He'd made several running comebacks and was training for the Boston Marathon. He was an active member of a local running club.

I reached out to his wife Cathi and we made plans to meet. She told me that one December evening, Denny didn't feel well after his daily run. He tried to analyze why he was so tired and couldn't figure it out. That same evening, he died of a heart attack.

Cathi told me that after Denny passed, she found a box containing many running race T-shirts and made a quilt out of them. She brought the quilt along and spread it onto the floor, asking if I could give her some history on the shirts. The quilt was amazing. I had memories about almost all the T-shirts. One that immediately caught my attention was the shirt that I had brought back for Denny from the National XC Championship in Burbank in 1982. I spent the next hour telling Cathi tales fueled by the T-shirts. The quilt did indeed tell a story—a story that ended much too soon, at age sixty-four.

When I think of the running world back in my hometown of Greenfield, I think of Ed Porter. Runners naturally are a fun bunch of people and Ed Porter was the king of fun. Ed was at the Y every day, a noontime runner and fitness enthusiast since coming to Greenfield in 1971.

I was always amazed at the range of Ed's ability. He was both a quarter- and half-miler in college, attending Washington and Jefferson College in Pennsylvania. Ed broke fifty seconds for the quarter and was a sub-two-minute half-miler. He told me that his coach unexpectedly put him in the two-mile race one day to replace an injured teammate…and he finished second! That's when Ed became hooked on distance running.

Despite getting the distance running bug, Ed didn't compete in a competitive race until 1975. Apparently, so the story goes, I convinced Ed to run the Amherst ten-mile road race with me. As Ed would be quoted as saying in a 1986 newspaper story, "Joe talked me into it, then he never showed up, but I ran it anyway."

Ed ran over twenty-five marathons. He actually had a streak, running Boston ten straight years. Ed joined us on many of our nightly running excursions as well as our long weekend runs. He was a fixture on the local road race scene and was a founding member of our local Greenfield running club, the Poet Seat Ridge Runners. Ed loved to have fun and he and his wife Corleen would regularly host post-race gatherings at their Madison Circle home. Ed was the life of the party. He had the best laugh!

Ed often traveled to races that he wasn't running, just to support his friends and provide water and moral support. Mickey Campaniello liked to tell the story of the time Ed parked in the Prudential Center garage. After running the marathon, he and Mickey couldn't remember where they left the car. After spending some time looking to no avail, they flagged down the security car and drove around till they spotted Ed's car.

Ed passed away from cancer in 1998. He left a lasting place in the hearts of so many.

It was April 19, 2017, when I heard the news that my friend Tom Fleming had died of a heart attack.

I was devastated and totally numb. The news rocked the whole running world. Tom was such a big part of so many lives. He was one of the world's best marathon runners and a great coach, teacher, father, and friend. Tom had a heart attack while doing what he loved best, coaching his Montclair Kimberly Academy track team. He was sixty-five years old.

I was honored to be asked to deliver a eulogy at Tom's memorial service in Montclair, New Jersey. The auditorium was standing-room only, with the overflow watching on a video screen in the school cafeteria. In attendance were Tom's family, his students, fellow teachers, his athletes, friends, and a remarkable gathering of individuals who made up a big piece of American distance running history.

Here is the eulogy I delivered:

> It is such an honor to have the opportunity to speak about my great friend, Tom.
>
> A Jewish friend of mine sent me an old Jewish saying: "May his memory be a blessing." What that really means, she explained, is that I'm wishing that the stories and recollections of Tom will influence all of us who knew him and encourage us to live better lives.
>
> I was at an event with Bill Rodgers before the Boston Marathon last year. I recognized Gloria Ratti, an institution with the Boston Athletic Association from what seems like the beginning of time. I went over and introduced myself. I told her I was a friend of Tom Fleming's. She smiled and said, "Tom, Tom; he is a good boy."
>
> Mrs. Fleming, you raised a good boy who became a great man!

Tom was all about family. He so loved his kids, Margot and Connor. You could always tell how much he loved his sister Joanne, just seeing them together. He thought the world of his brother-in-law, Tim. Tom called his mother every single day. He loved his dad, he missed him so much. He thanked his dad at his Distance Running Hall of Fame induction ceremony. Looking up to heaven he said, "Dad, we did it together." Tom is now with his dad.

Bloomfield, New Jersey: where it all started. It was a bit like Mr. Rogers'

Neighborhood. Through Tom, I met a whole host of characters. I met Mitch, Eddie Silverman, Brophy, Threadgold, Alden, Alexandra, Jeff Benjamin, and Don Adjean. Tom talked about Connelly, Reilly, and really so many of you I can't even mention now. Sometimes after an event when Tom was out celebrating with his buddies, he'd call me and put them on the phone. I'd never met them, but there I was, talking to guys like Jeff Hartke. I learned about the diner, Town Pub, Lombardi's, and Fitzgerald's. Tom was all Bloomfield, all Jersey, right to the core. I don't think he ever lived more than two miles from where he grew up.

Tom loved the Yankees and he despised the Red Sox. I love the Red Sox, and the Yankees…well, you can guess. I can assure you that I would never do this for anyone else but Tom, as I put on this Yankees hat. On our granddaughter's first day of school, I texted Tom a picture of her wearing her new Red Sox backpack.

Less than a minute later, Tom responded back, "What is that? A parachute for when the Red Sox take their big fall in September?"

Tom loved the Boston Celtics and Larry Bird. I think his fantasy was to play for the Celtics. We had a mutual friend, Milt Borofsky, who had the best seats in the Old Boston Garden. Tom would even fly up on People's Express for a game. I would pick him up at the airport and we would go to the game. Afterwards, I would bring him back to the airport. One night, we were going to dinner after the game. He told me that he would meet me at the restaurant. A half hour later, Tom marched into the restaurant with the entire NBA officiating crew including his buddy, veteran official Bob Delaney. It caused quite a stir as the patrons had just finished watching the game on the bar television.

Traditions were big with Tom, Bill and I. We formed a small group and for years we would go to the Millrose Games at Madison Square Garden. We called ourselves "the Millrose Six." Bill Rodgers, Fred Doyle, Rick Sherlund, Jon Barnes, Tom, and me. Being with Tom and Bill meant we always had people coming by our seats to say hello. Between the two of them, it seemed like they knew half of the people in the Garden.

One visitor was Olympic gold medal sprinter Dennis Mitchell. Dennis sat next to me for a while and told me that even though he was a sprinter and Tom a distance runner, Tom was his role model growing up. He told me how much he admired Tom's work ethic. Dennis was dressed to the max: black shirt, red tie, velour black jacket, black dress pants, and white shoes. There was a brief lull in the action as Dennis was walking back to his seat. The Garden was quiet for a moment. Tom yelled out, "Dennis, next time ask before you take clothes from my closet!"

Bill, Tom, and I were like the Three Amigos. We loved having fun and laughing together. We had so many memorable adventures.

Our most favorite tradition together was New Year's. Tom would come up every year, usually two or three days in advance. He would assist my wife Ginger with opening cans of ingredients to make the chili. Tom would help get the house ready for our open house on New Year's Day. He loved to operate the vacuum cleaner. Tom had, let's just say, an abundance of energy. On New Year's Day, Tom would greet our guests at the door just like it was his own party.

I had to keep him busy, so I took him to work with me. Once, we had construction meeting regarding my new Y. Tom told me he would sit in the meeting and just observe. There was an issue with the project when Tom stepped in and said, "We had the same problem at the Montclair Kimberly Academy, let me tell you how we resolved it." The construction superintendent asked who he was and if he was a project manager. He replied, "I'm Tom from Jersey. I'm a teacher and a coach."

I hardly said a word in the whole meeting. Tom just took right over. Tom so loved to coach. Coaching became his calling. A few weeks ago, we were talking about coaching and Tom said to me, "It's all about passion and desire to achieve. You can talk it up as a coach…but you can't coach it!" Jackie Hanson, one of our truly great American woman marathon runners, sent me a few paragraphs about Tom and asked that I share them.

From Jackie:

At the Cleveland Marathon, we won together, but the mayor of Cleveland, Dennis Kucinich, was ill-informed and brought just one key to the city at the awards ceremony. Since Tom was traveling home the same day and I was staying one more day, I suggested he take the key, since I could receive mine the next day.

Nearly forty years later, I would still be waiting for my key, despite the good intentions of a reporter who put the story out into the news on one of Cleveland Marathon's anniversaries.

Well, Tom learned of the story and resolved the situation in his own generous way. He sent the key to me recently, saying after all this time, it was my turn to keep it for the next thirty-plus years. The key to my heart.

What a gentleman.

What a competitor.

What a team player.

What a friend.

I will miss him, but I have a cherished key and a treasure trove of memories.

JH

As I close this morning, I would like to share a few lines from a Dennis Wilson song:
"Farewell my friend
My beautiful friend
Farewell
You take the high road
And I'll take the low road
And we'll meet again.
Farewell my friend."
Here's to Denny, Ed, and Tom.

20

Laughing All the Way

Bill Rodgers and I were driving back from visiting a friend, traveling east on Route 2. We started talking about getting a quick bite to eat and a beer. I knew just the place, a nice tavern located in a beautiful inn.

I knew the place well, as it was the location of my daughter Marjorie and her husband Jason's wedding rehearsal dinner. Bill had been to the tavern with me before and agreed it was the perfect place to stop. We parked the car and went up to the door. The door, for some reason, was locked or stuck as I tried it several times. A few seconds later, a woman dressed in business attire along with a big guy opened the door and asked if she could help us. I told her we were looking to have a few beers in the tavern. She sternly said, "There is no tavern here!" and abruptly shut the door on us.

Bill and I shrugged our shoulders, speechless, and headed back to our car. I looked up at the sign, which was in the exact spot as it had always been. I did a double take—the inn was now a drug and alcohol rehabilitation center! There we were, banging on the rehab door, telling them we needed a beer.

We laughed all the way home wondering what the people were thinking about us!

My friend Wayne Westcott, fitness author and speaker, used to travel almost as much as Bill Rodgers. Wayne called to tell me that he ran into Bill at the airport. I wasn't sure why that was worthy of a phone call until Wayne told me the whole story.

Wayne was going through security at Boston Logan Airport when all of a sudden, this guy threw his things down in front of Wayne's bag on the X-ray machine and slid quickly by, obviously in a big hurry. As the gentleman picked up his bag, Wayne recognized him and yelled out to him. Bill looked up and said, "Can't talk, Wayne, I have to get on my flight!" and off he jogged, full-speed toward his gate.

The security guy said to Wayne, "He'll never make it."

"Of course he will," Wayne replied. "That's Bill Rodgers, the best marathon runner in the world!"

The security agent responded, "I don't care who he is—the plane left ten minutes ago."

Tom Fleming, Bill Rodgers, and I were on a hot summer run from my apartment in Natick. The ten-mile loop went right by the Massachusetts women's prison in Framingham. As we ran by the prison, Tom noticed the women were out in the yard for recreation. Tom had the loudest New Jersey two-finger whistle and got the inmates' attention. The yard grew quiet and Tom yelled out, "Ladies, here he is, the king of the roads, the king!" The women began to whistle at Bill, who was shirtless, along with quite a few "hey baby"-type comments. Bill picked up the pace to get by the prison but I swear he had a smile on his face!

Bill and I were on an afternoon training run in Sherborn, Mass. We were running along an area with high grass reaching to the edge of the road. All of a sudden, we heard rustling in the grass and out came an Irish Setter. The dog proceeded to run with us, lagging behind at times and then sprinting by us. At first, we thought it was funny, we had a new training partner. As the run went on, the dog darted out into the road, causing cars to honk their horns. People rolled down their windows and yelled, "Get your freakin' dog out of the road!" Naturally, everyone thought it was our dog.

This went on for two days, causing a lot of stress. We kept thinking there was no way the dog would show up again, but sure enough, he reappeared like magic. It was like he knew our schedule.

On the third day, the dog again appeared, running in and out of the road with the cars honking at us. As the dog sprinted up ahead, Bill and I took a quick turn down a side road, running at full speed. We ditched him!

The next day we were on our run when we looked ahead and saw the dog coming at us. We both said out loud, "Oh no!" When the dog got up to us, he looked straight ahead and kept going by us like we weren't even there. It was like he was saying, "F you, guys!" We never saw that dog again.

Growing up as a high school student, my father was the superintendent of the Franklin County House of Correction. My father's responsibilities included being on call twenty-four/seven. Because of this, my family lived in an apartment connected to the prison. It was a unique place to grow up, to say the least. It was fun seeing the look on a date's face when I said I needed to stop home for a minute, pressing the intercom button and waiting for the prison gate to open.

One evening, my father told me about some musicians from UMass who were coming to entertain the inmates. He said they played guitars and harmonicas and invited me to attend. I took my place behind the bars in the administration area.

The trio of musicians was greeted warmly by the inmates and the performance began. From my view from behind the bars, I could mostly see the performers from the side.

After one of the songs, one of the guys from the band turned my way. I did a double take—it was Tom Derderian! Tom was an early running mentor of mine. I had no idea he played the guitar and he had no idea I lived in a prison. We both stared at each other in bewilderment.

At the end of the concert, Tom came over and asked what I was doing there. I told him my story and we both got quite a laugh. Over the years, we often joke about the night we spent behind bars together! Always fun to see the reaction of those around us.

21

The Finish Line

Running has been a big part of my life since I was fourteen years old. I truly value the friendships and relationships I've made along the way. I treasure the early days when Frank McDonald and I were starting out in the sport. Everything was so simple and new. We were young and constantly seeking ways to become better at training.

The New York City Marathon with Rick Sherlund in 1970 was very special. The New York Road Runners Club honored the Class of 1970 at the twenty-fifth reunion in 1989. I'll never forget the twenty-four-hour relay and how challenging it was. I can still recall running around the board track in the old Boston Garden and hearing Coach Conway yelling to me to, "Keep contact with that guy!" I truly value the memories I had coaching the Greenfield High School girls' track team and winning the Western Mass title. I treasure the unforgettable experience of being on the staff at the Bill Rodgers Running and Fitness Camps with Tom Fleming, Greg Meyers, Joan Benoit Samuelson, and Nancy Clark, and the guest appearance of Dr. George Sheehan, the running guru of our sport in the early days.

I remember how motivated I was going on a few runs with Dave Ciszewski, who was the top runner on the Greenfield High School cross-country team. Tom Derderian was a top runner at UMass and a really good road runner. He'd often talk with me about training and racing. On the national/international level, I was influenced by Peter Snell, George Young, Steve Prefontaine, Jim Ryun, Marty Liquori, and Gerry Lindgren.

I absolutely loved to compete. In high school, my two toughest competitors were Bobby Williams from Pioneer Regional High School and Mike Connelly from Turners Falls High School. On the roads, Steve Snover, Russ Holt, John Jarek, Bobby Neil, Tom Derderian, Denny Tetreault, and Ken Kaczenski were super tough runners. Although Denny never beat me under a half-marathon distance, he always made his presence known. Russ Holt was a veteran road runner in my early days. As a seventeen-year-old senior, I finally beat Russ to win the Holyoke/Bathe Shoppe race. Russ was so angry, he wouldn't come to the podium to accept his award! Ken was tough as nails, a super runner, and an amazing talent.

I competed in cross-country, track, and road racing. All three are unique and special in their own ways. I loved road races best. Road racing has been extremely popular in New England since the 1950s. Ever since my first race in Granby in 1966, I was hooked. On many weekends, there would be four or five races to choose from. Races were mainly five-, six-, and ten-milers in those days. It seemed like most towns had a race on the schedule at some point during the year. In the early days, races were sanctioned by the Amateur Athletic Union, which meant you had to have a membership card to compete. The rules and regulations were ridiculous. I remember Boston Marathon champion Amby Burfoot once wore a white painter's hat to protect him from the sun and the AAU officials made Amby turn the hat inside out so that no advertising was visible. Fortunately, these archaic rules began to change.

Author John Jerome describes the moment that everything comes together and you have a great performance as "the sweet spot in time." They don't come along often, but fortunately, I did have a few. Four of them stick out in my mind.

In 1981, I won and set a course record in the West Springfield/Galaska 6.8-mile road race. I ran alone from the start and remember the gun going off and Ed Porter yelling, "See you later, Joe."

I set my personal record and a course record at the 5K West Newton/Troubadour Trot in 1986. I ran 14:35 and ran alone after the first mile.

In 1982, I led the Hyannis Johnny Kelly Half-Marathon for 11.5 miles before I was overtaken. I ended up in second place but felt it was one of my top performances. I remember that the finish line announcer for WCOD was Rick Walters, originally from Greenfield.

But if I could only pick one "sweet spot in time," I'd have to pick winning the Western Mass High School two-mile. It was a very hot, dry day and the two-mile was the last event. The cinder track was full of ruts from the heavy usage that day. Coach Conway called the condition of the track "a dust bowl." After the first lap, I ran alone and the crowd was really supportive. I set the Western Mass record and felt that I could have run much faster if I was pushed. I remember my father being there and cheering me on.

Reflecting back, I think my training plans were always pretty solid. My typical training was seventy-five to eighty-five miles per week. I did some higher mileage, running between a hundred and a hundred ten miles per week, but I found it too tough for my body. My most important day was my "quality workout" at the track, on the roads, or at the cemetery. My favorite workouts were three-times-one mile in 4:50 and five-times-1K in 2:58. I always tried to simulate racing conditions in those workouts.

Another favorite was an eight-mile run in the Greenfield Meadows, with a 4:45 mile in the middle. I usually did one longer run of thirteen to eighteen miles, followed by easy recovery runs of eight to ten miles the rest of the week. I emphasize "easy," as I know many runners who leave their best efforts on the road in training.

The training did take a toll, physically. I think I could write a book on running injuries. Unfortunately, I never had a lightweight running body. I was running fit and lean at 150 pounds on a short muscular frame. My most nagging injuries were plantar fasciitis, sciatica, torn meniscus, and tendinitis in the ball of my foot. The injury that caused me to stop competing was an arthritic/frozen toe.

In the early days, prizes consisted of trophies and medals. I have quite a collection in boxes in the basement. In the late seventies, merchandise prizes became popular. You would check out the prizes before the race so that when they called you up, you knew what was on the table.

I won a ten-speed bike, restaurant gift certificates, a coffee table, wine, a camera, groceries, running shoes, even a carpet. After winning the original Shelburne road race, I was presented with a gift certificate for a case of beer and a bottle of gin! Unfortunately, it was a Sunday and package stores were closed back then. I always enjoyed my arrangement with Jack Sullivan, the owner of Joe's Café in Northampton. A win with a Joe's T-shirt on would mean free pizza and beer!

The biggest reward of all is the people I have met on the way. I made them a big part of this book because they played a big role in my running life.

Long may you run.

Running Résumé

Greenfield High School Cross-Country Highlights

XC Dual Meets: twenty-one

Nineteen wins and seven course records

Undefeated on the home course

Western Mass 1967: sixth place

Western Mass 1968: second place

Western Mass 1969: first place

Western Mass course record: 1969

Greenfield High School Track Highlights

Western Mass 1968: one-mile outdoor champion

Western Mass 1970: one-mile indoor champion

Western Mass 1970: two-mile indoor champion

Western Mass 1970: two-mile outdoor champion (Western Mass record)

1970 State Indoor: two-mile runner-up

Road Race Highlights

WAQY Road Race, Springfield: third place

Johnny Kelly Half-Marathon, Hyannis: second place

Holyoke/Bathe Shoppe Road Race: first place

Mike Hanlon Twenty-Miler, NYC: first place, teenage division

NYC Marathon: thirteenth place

West Springfield Road Race: first place

Don Nardi/Agawam Road Race: first place

Hampshire Gazette/Northampton Road Race: first place

Montague/Mug Race: first place

Newton/Troubadour Trot: first place

Career Summary

Two hundred twenty-five races run (cross-country, track, and road races)

Ninety-six wins

64,280 training miles run

Acknowledgments

So many people played a role in my development as a runner and as a person.

Jim Allen: friend, mentor and YMCA legend (RIP 2000).

Stan Benjamin: ninth grade gym teacher; encouraged me to go out for cross-country (RIP 2009).

Mickey Campaniello: friend and running partner, marathoner and beyond.

Dave Ciszewski: early running mentor and friend.

Don Clark: my boss at Clark's Sport Shop, long-time supporter and friend.

Pete "Coach" Conway: my high school track coach, mentor, and friend.

Nancy Conz: friend and Twosome relay partner, winner of the Chicago and Ottawa Marathons (RIP 2017).

Carry Crossman: friend and training partner (RIP 2005).

Tom Derderian: coach of the Greater Boston Track Club, early mentor, author, and life-long running friend.

Fred Doyle: friend and training partner, member of the Millrose Six; ran for the University of New Hampshire.

Tom Fleming: dear friend, running legend, and one of the Three Amigos; member of the Millrose Six; two-time winner of the New York City Marathon and twice runner-up of the Boston Marathon (RIP 2017).

Ken Kaczenski: friend and training partner; All-American at Northeastern University, affectionately known as "The Rookie" (RIP 2012).

Rich Kells: my tennis coach (RIP 2020).

Jack Mahurin: friend and training partner.

Frank McDonald: lifelong friend and my original running partner; we started this journey together fifty-four years ago! Frank ran track and cross-country for Providence College.

Paul McDonald: early running and tennis mentor and friend; my father's doubles partner; Western Mass high school champion in the mile and tennis singles in the same season, ran for Springfield College.

Jim Murphy, friend and training partner, artist extraordinaire.

Coach Ken O'Brien: UMass track and cross-country coach.

Ed Porter: friend, training partner, and fellow member of the Poet Seat Ridge Runners (RIP 1996).

Connie Putnam: training partner, friend, and former coach at Tufts University.

Roger Reid: training partner and friend.

Bill Rodgers: friend, training partner, and one of the Three Amigos, member of the Millrose Six; four-time winner of the Boston and New York City Marathons; a genuine legend.

Rick Sherlund: training partner, my best man, and fellow member of the New York City Marathon Class of 1970 and member of the Millrose Six; our many adventures together could fill their own book.

Peter Stasz: president of the Greater Springfield Harriers, friend, and fellow competitor.

Denny Tetreault: friend, training partner, and competitor; one of the toughest runners on the road (RIP 2012).

Ed Walkwitz: early training partner, marathon runner, and former national 50K champion.

Peter Wayman: high school teammate and friend.

Wayne Westcott: friend and fitness author/speaker; former runner at Penn State.

My family, for all your loving support: Ginger Martino, my wife and rock. Joe Martino, Sr. (father), Barbara Martino (stepmom), Hileary Cleary (daughter), Neil Cleary (son-in-law), Grace Cleary (granddaughter), Lily Cleary (granddaughter), Marjorie Heim (daughter), Jason Heim (son-in-law), Jacob Heim (grandson), Addie Heim (granddaughter), Harper Heim (granddaughter), Greg Martino (brother), Tony Martino (brother), Sue Martino (sister-in-law), Megan Martino (niece), Benjamin Martino (nephew).

Special thanks Kevin LeBlanc for his help producing this book, Linda Heim for editing all the photographs, and to Ana Gabriel Mann (née Ruth Ann Burt) and her husband, John David Mann, for their willingness to take the baton and shepherd this project to the finish line!

About the Author

Joe Martino discovered his passion at the age of fourteen, when he ran his first race. During his high school years he set multiple course and track records, including winning the 1969 Western Mass cross-country championship and the 1970 Western Mass two-mile, and went on to run a career total of 255 races with 96 first-place finishes. During those years he also formed close friendships with two of America's greatest distance runners, Bill Rodgers and Tom Fleming. (The three friends called themselves "the Three Amigos.")

Joe is a graduate of the University of Massachusetts, Amherst, where he majored in Physical Education. In 1982 he began a thirty-four year career working for the YMCA organization, during which time he became a leader in the Y wellness movement, leading workshops and training around the country. He retired in 2016 and spends time with family, gardening, playing tennis and sailing his boat *Sundance*. Joe lives in Medway, Massachusetts, with his wife Ginger.

Made in the USA
Columbia, SC
29 November 2020